I0071544

CommonWealth
An Introduction to
Business Economics

This introduction to business economics has been written by an accountant with a master's degree in accountancy (1980) and a Ph.D. in business administration (1983) from the AACSB accredited Sam Walton College of the University of Arkansas, USA.

The book is designed to present a broad international framework of business economics. Written from the position of a libertarian free-marketeer, it explains how businesses develop and the legal, financial framework within which they need to achieve growth.

LIFE OF DREW CARSON

Sam Drew Carson was born in the North of Ireland and educated there at Wellington College and the Ulster Polytechnic. He completed his education in the USA at New Mexico Highlands University and the University of Arkansas and has traveled widely in North America, around the Atlantic and in Europe.

Drew worked as a seaman and fish-gutter in Vestmannaeyjar off the coast of Iceland. He lived and worked in the Irish and Western Isles Gaeltachts and was married in Welsh-speaking Carmarthen after which he honeymooned in Belfast.

He has told his stories, composed and sung his songs, seeking storylines in Bristol and the English Westcountry. Drew has also lived and written in Nashville, Tennessee, in the wooded hills of Mid-America and from the Appalachians to the Ozarks. This was the culture that gave rise to the now worldwide Scotch-Irish country music.

In the USA, he also worked beside the bayous of the French-speaking Cajuns in the South and among the Western Spanish-speaking Navajos, Apaches and Pueblos of the Sangre de Cristo Mountains in New Mexico.

Drew has sailed far into the seas of old Gaelic and Oriental legend. After many years searching for inspiration for story and music, the author is still traveling and writing.

BOOKS BY THE SAME AUTHOR
available from - www.createspace.com

SAGA OF TSUNAMI –
the Trilogy, 2nd edition
ISBN: 978-0-9561435-1-8

ZENISUB –
Fun and Games in Businezz
ISBN: 978-0-9561435-2-5

GOOD FOR A LAUGH –
Six Funny Playscripts for Amateurs
ISBN: 978-0-9561435-3-2

HOME WITH A GOOD COMPANION –
Amateur Pantomime Scripts for a Merry Winter
ISBN: 978-0-9561435-4-9

BACK TO THE GOOD OLD DAYS –
Miracle Plays of Sunlight and Shadow
ISBN: 978-0-9561435-5-6

CLASSIC EUROPEAN LYRICS –
*Translated from the Gaelic, the French and
the Spanish*
ISBN: 978-0-9561435-6-3

COMMONWEALTH –
An Introduction to Business Economics
ISBN: 978-0-9561435-7-0

COMMONWEALTH

AN INTRODUCTION TO
BUSINESS ECONOMICS

DREW CARSON

Order from:
https://www.createspace.com/3677275

Legals

© Copyright, Samuel Andrew Carson, 2012
All rights reserved.
Published by S. A. Carson,
29 Northleaze, Long Ashton, Bristol BS41 9HS, UK
Publisher's email: verygoodreading@googlemail.com

The right of Dr. S. A. Carson, to be identified as the author of
this work, has been asserted.

ISBN: 978-0-9561435-7-0

TABLE OF CONTENTS

PAGE

Chapter One

INTRODUCTION 13

Chapter Two

SWOPSHOP..17

    Betweentaking 17

    Entrepreneurial Development 18

Chapter Three

ARBITRAGE..21

    Markets 21

    Scarcity or Rarity...21

    Arbitrage...22

    Creative Arbitrage 23

Chapter Four

DEMAND AND SUPPLY 25

    Demand and Price 25

    The Supply Curve 25

    The Demand Curve...27

Chapter Five

EQUILIBRIUM 28

    Cross Purposes 28

    Compromise...29

    Imbalances...31

    Special Information 32

Chapter Six

INFLATION 35

    Supply, Demand and Money..35

    What Causes Inflation?...35

    What Causes Deflation? 39

Chapter Seven

INFLATION AND THE MARKETPLACE 41

    An Overheated Economy?..41

    Oversupplies 42

    Shortages...43

Chapter Eight

THE GROWTH OF MONEY 45

    Behavioral Theory of Money 45

    Public Support...46

    The Government Money Wheel.....................................46

    The Multiplier...47

    The Entrepreneurial Boomerang.................................49

Chapter Nine

MARKETS.. 55

    Different Markets 55

    Supply and the Market.................................... 56

Chapter Ten

THE SAPLING FOREST 57

    Business Risk 57

    Economic Growth 58

    Small Growth Upwards................................... 59

    Historical Precedent 60

    The Up-Down Theories 61

    Growth of Wealth 62

    Growth-Upwards Theory of Money 63

Chapter Eleven

PYRAMID OF PROFITS 65

    Basic Market.. 67

    Purpose of Basic Market 68

    The Middle-Level Markets 69

    The Higher-Level Market................................ 69

    Support for Basic Markets 70

    Top-Down Support 71

    Top-Down Revolution 71

    Neither Loans Nor Handouts........................... 72

Chapter Twelve

BUSINESS PREDICTIONS 75

    The Fourth Factor.. 75

    Non-Predictable Models 76

    Model Fanatics 77

    Statistics Not Math... 79

    The Best Factor of Production......................... 80

Chapter Thirteen

CONDITIONS FOR GROWTH 82

    Fifteen Conditions Favorable to Entrepreneurship.......... 82

Chapter Fourteen

BUSINESS RIGHTS AND CONDITIONS 88

    Which Rights or Conditions? 88

    Libertarian Conditions.................................... 89

    A Model Bill of Business Rights?..................... 90

    Fewer and Fairer Laws................................... 91

Chapter Fifteen

MORAL RIGHTS 95

    Free Speech 96

Free Press...97
Right to Walk...99
Right to Know or Hear the Truth 100
Religion 101
Effective Public Spending 103
Meritocracy...104

Chapter Sixteen

SECURITY RIGHTS 112
Auditing of Public Purse..112
Law and Order 116
Liberty and Life 117
Peace...118
Privacy 119
Integration 120
Personal Protection...121

Chapter Seventeen

POLITICAL RIGHTS 122
Citizenship..122
Checks and Balances 125
Three Levels of Democracy 125
Fair Voting..128
Direct Choice of Leaders 129
Fair Press...129
Recall of Failures 130

Chapter Eighteen

FINANCIAL RIGHTS...132
Good Wages 132
Free Business Entry...135
A Market Economy...142
Effective Taxes 146
Balanced Interest Rates..149
Receive Debts Owed 151
Fair Shares for All 152

Chapter Nineteen

SOCIAL RIGHTS 156
Public Education 156
Land Reform 161
A Pension...162
Public Communications 162
Public Transit 164
Co-ops..164
Travel 167

Chapter Twenty

JUDICIAL RIGHTS.. 169
    Presumption of Innocence... 169
    Equality... 170
    Laws of Fairness 171
    Fair Trials.. 173
    Victim's Compensation.. 174
    Free Courts.. 175
    Accountable Governments 176

Chapter Twenty One

PERSONAL RIGHTS... 177
    Buy a Home... 177
    Ownership of Assets.. 179
    Self-Defense.. 179
    Ownership of Ideas.. 181
    Public Healthcare 183
    Human Self-Reliance... 185
    Individual Choices 185

Chapter Twenty Two

SUMMARY 187

PART I
SUPPLY AND DEMAND

INTRODUCTION
THE SWOPSHOP
ARBITRAGE
DEMAND AND SUPPLY
EQUILIBRIUM

An Old Proverb says:
Some do buy and sell
And live by the loss

CHAPTER ONE
INTRODUCTION

This book is a primer on business and economics. It covers the economic and political aspects of business, including wealth creation and growth from essentially a libertarian free market viewpoint. The book emphasizes the ability to make business decisions without the constraints of government regulations and guidelines.

There are three ways to achieve a fair spread of money:

1. **Socialism** – the management of large sums of money by central government.
2. **Capitalism** – the organization of large amounts of money by private firms.
3. **CommonWealthism** – the encouragement of a fair spread of money by participation in co-ops, private businesses, partnerships and entrepreneurship within a framework of free markets. That is, a business law-based commonwealth with business-friendly human rights.

Most economies today employ all three methods. This book will look at ideas about commonwealthism. It should be understood that the creation of wealth cannot be achieved effectively by either socialism or capitalism alone. So it is important to understand how commonwealthism can work for society and individuals.

Some of the main topics dealt with will include:

1. Business creates wealth.
2. Business should be organized in a structured and methodical way.
3. Business law sets out the framework for business rules and responsibilities.
4. Good business law provides a predictable and reliable background for the conduct of business.
5. Good business law should incorporate the rights and freedoms of the business manager within a legal structure of commonwealthism.

The creation of wealth often represented by money, the creation of moniesworth, entails the development of land, labor and capital into coherent businesses by the business manager or entrepreneur who is the overall organizer of the firm.

This book will also discuss the creation of business firms and the business-friendly political framework which needs to define the legal and structured environment.

The following topics will be discussed:

- CommonWealthism
- Growth of Markets
- Growth of Money
- Business Rights such as:

   Moral

   Security

   Political

   Financial

   Social

   Judicial

   Personal

This book is merely a primer, an introduction to the basics of business. So, for the sake of simplicity, business is here set out as one discipline which includes economics. Of course, if one wishes, separate specializations may be developed at a later stage, such as:

Introduction

- Finance
- Accounting
- Marketing
- Behavioral Management
- Information Systems
- Statistics

CommonWealthism

The growth and fair spread of money by means of private businesses, partnerships and co-ops.

CHAPTER TWO
THE SWOPSHOP

Traditionally, Land, Labor, Capital and Entrepreneurship have been accepted as the four factors of production and the basis of business growth. There is very little in the way of economic theory that is necessary for successful business management beyond the basic principles of the child's swopshop.

Betweentaking

Betweentaking is the function of the entrepreneur in achieving a profit between buying and selling of goods or services.

The economics of BETWEENTAKING is that of the child's swopshop. Beg, borrow or steal a few foods, toys or cards or stamps, swop them for more or better odds and ends from children who want a change of toy, due to boredom, sales-talk, fashion, desire to imitate or occasionally - need. TAKE any profits that occur BETWEEN these deals.

In fact, the child's swopshop in more sophisticated form leads on to the four factors of production.

> **The child's swopshop
> is the pattern of all business.**

> **The entrepreneur is a magician who adds
> 3 + 3 and gets the answer 7
> – a very lucky number.**

Entrepreneurial Development

For business to succeed and that also means for any economy to grow overall, the four factors of production must all be working together as follows:

1. **Land** - this includes the rule of law and order and all necessary permissions to use the land and premises in peace and in good order with all communications.

2. **Labor** - skilled and unskilled but routine. This includes all those who do a routine job - managerial or technical or manual - under the direction of a supervisor (or board) and according to a set pattern or job description or learned body of knowledge. Labor, skilled or not, ranges downwards from chief executive officer and includes all specialized divisional directors such as:

- Finance,
- Production,
- Marketing and Sales,
- Human Resources,
- Foreign Sales,
- Training and Education,
- Distribution,
- Computers - Communications.

3. **Capital** - equipment, plant, tools, software and information also including processes and communications systems needed to carry out the business.

4. **Entrepreneur** - The business manager or entrepreneur brings together the other three factors with their numberless subsections and moulds them into that productive synergistic machine known as a business or a firm. Thus, the true business manager is a magician, an alchemist who turns base metals into silver and gold - a lucky person with a lucky role to play and a destiny to bring jobs and pensions and profit and value-added wealth to himself and to the community.

The four factors of production are:
Land
Labor
Capital
Entrepreneurship/Business Management

Only the basic laws of supply and demand including the circular flow of goods actually apply in ordinary entrepreneurial situations, as opposed to specialized entrepreneurs who are, for instance, currency or commodity or stock or bond traders.

These basic laws of supply and demand are of the essence of business management. The following chapters will examine in more detail these laws of supply and demand and the concept of arbitrage.

CHAPTER THREE
ARBITRAGE

Markets

A market is a place where goods (including services) are bought and sold. For example – The Farmers' Market or the Stock Market.

Scarcity or Rarity

To be valuable a good must be rare or scarce. Air is plentiful above ground and cannot be sold - there is a limitless supply of air so that it has no value.

However, underneath the sea, air is scarce so that it can be sold in canisters for the use of scubadivers. Air has value under the water because there it is scarce.

All goods, similarly, have value because of their scarcity. Gold is rare and therefore is valuable. Drinking water has some scarcity but, compared to gold, it is plentiful and so has a low value.

Scarcity often depends on the place or location of the commodity since it can be plentiful in one place and rare in another. Scarcity is therefore the basis of arbitrage.

Arbitrage

Arbitrage is buying assets at lower prices where money is scarce and selling them at higher prices where money is more plentiful.

A simple example of basic entrepreneurship or arbitrage would be to buy gold in Slum-Town and sell it in Snob-Town. The business manager takes the difference which is usually a small profit.

Arbitrage also operates where money is scarce for the purchase of goods or commodities or antiques in a poor area but money is slightly more forthcoming for such items in uptown London or New York.

Once again the business manager buys low, sells high and TAKES the difference BETWEEN the two markets.

This classical arbitrage consists of simply moving goods from where they are cheap to where they are expensive.

ARBITRAGE
Arbitrage is buying assets at lower prices
where money is scarce
and selling them at higher prices
where money is more plentiful.

Art and jewelry are plentiful where artists live but more rare where there are fewer artists. So, entrepreneurs known as arbitrageurs travel to Santa Fe, New Mexico; USA or Africa or the Far East to buy works of art and then take them to London or New York or wherever there is a high-demand market (or scarcity premium). They then sell the artworks at a profit - high enough to cover their expenses and more.

The entrepreneur TAKES the difference in price BETWEEN the plentiful markets (at a low price) and the scarcity market (at a higher price).

'entre' = between and 'prendre' = to take

ARBITRAGE EXAMPLE
When air is moved from the surface to underwater, the increase in value is called arbitrage.

Creative Arbitrage

Another form of arbitrage is for a famous singer to buy a song from an unknown author. The singer gives the song a good recording and makes an income from the royalties. In this case the singer's talent and fame play the same part as distance, time, processing or labor in other forms of arbitrage. The original songwriter should also benefit from the newly acquired fame.

Gene Autry, the singing cowboy, was a business manager of this type whose genius lay in recognizing good songs while they were still unknown. Then Gene paid a fair price for the song and recorded it. Some of the songwriters also became millionaires due to the increased recognition of their talents whereby they got higher prices for later songs. Everybody was happy including Gene's fans, like the present author.

The same principle applies to books published or works of art added to famous collections.

CREATIVE ARBITRAGE
A work of art is moved from a simple to a more sophisticated market.

The concepts of supply and demand will now be examined in more detail.

CHAPTER FOUR
DEMAND AND SUPPLY

Demand and Price

One of the two basic laws of economics is the law of demand. The law is a principle or general tendency in markets that BUYERS WILL DEMAND MORE AS PRICE DECLINES.

More people will normally demand any given good or service or product at a lower price than at a higher price. This is because most people are poor and only a few people are rich. Assuming that the product is a desirable one for many, it follows that more people can afford to buy it at the lower price.

LAW OF DEMAND
The law of demand states that
buyers will normally demand more
as price declines.

The Supply Curve

Again, the great tendency of SUPPLIERS is for producers (or other sellers) to supply more when prices are higher in order to get a bigger profit. Farmers will wish to grow more potatoes when the price of potatoes is higher. Importers of computers will buy and import more computers when demand is high and prices are higher. When winter clothes are in demand and prices of woolies are high, producers will put on an extra shift or even expand their production looms to produce more and so sell at higher than normal prices.

A supply curve would illustrate this general tendency for producers/suppliers to try to sell more when prices are high.

Such a curve would be a picture, a drawing of human behavior which tends to sell more willingly at higher prices (e.g., 8000 items would be supplied at 6 dollars each) and conversely to sell less and less willingly at lower prices (3000 items would be supplied - and offered for sale - at say 4 dollars each). A curve line would represent the amount supplied at various prices.

LAW OF SUPPLY
The Law of Supply states that
suppliers will tend to supply more
when prices are higher to get a bigger profit.

The Demand Curve

A demand curve is sometimes used to illustrate the fact that there is a general tendency for people to buy more as the price comes down. Such a curve would illustrate a picture of human behavior.

It would show that people tend to buy less at higher prices (e.g., 400 items at 3 euros each) and similarly to buy more at lower prices (e.g., 1000 items at 1 euro each).

The curve line would represent the amounts bought at the various prices or currency units such as dollars, pounds or euros.

Likewise, a demand curve could be drawn showing the greater demand for products at the lower prices.

There is a greater tendency for suppliers to sell at the higher prices. It follows therefore that these two behaviors will meet at a point of compromise where (in theory) all sellers will sell and all buyers will buy.

SUPPLIERS will tend to *sell* more at *higher prices*.
BUYERS will tend to *buy* more at *lower prices*.

These statements are an outline of the Laws of Supply and Demand.

CHAPTER FIVE
EQUILIBRIUM

Cross Purposes

Now arises a problem - the tendencies of people to buy and sell are moving in opposite directions and are, in fact, in direct opposition to each other.

Sellers are digging old furniture out of the attic to plonk it in the yard sale when the town is full of new arrivals. The new arrivals, in turn, are searching the yard sales and flea markets for the cheapest furniture they can find.

- Sellers wish to sell at higher prices.
- Buyers want to buy only at lower prices.
- Both cannot get their way.
- Both cannot succeed fully at the same time since buyers and sellers are, in general, pulling in opposite directions.
- Buyers want to buy cheap but suppliers and sellers want to sell at higher prices.

So what happens? What happens is what usually happens when rational people disagree - there is a compromise between those who want to sell at high prices and those who wish to buy at low prices.

Compromise

In fact, in theory, if people are rational (and of course they rarely are) there is always a price, a point of compromise (or equilibrium) where suppliers are prepared to sell and buyers are prepared to buy.

In practice, people are never consistently rational. This point of balance where buyers and sellers agree is really more of an area than an exact figure.

Yet, the theory points to a tendency which is very true to life. There is always a movement towards a point where sellers will sell and buyers will buy - since sellers cannot eat all their potatoes themselves and buyers must eat something and why not good cheap potatoes?

Likewise, a drawing could be made of the equilibrium point where buyers and sellers would come together and where products will clear the decks at a price of, for instance, 3 pounds and a quantity of 6 million.

Equilibrium

> ## EQUILIBRIUM
> **There is always a price,
> a point of compromise, or equilibrium,
> where suppliers are prepared to sell
> and buyers are prepared to buy.**

In practice, as opposed to theory, again, this equilibrium point represents a general tendency for people to meet each other half-way on matters of buying and selling.

In general, too, when prices are above this equilibrium point, fewer buyers will pay the high prices and so there will be an excess or surplus of products that lie on the shelves unsold.

Similarly, in general, when prices are below the equilibrium there will be a tendency of suppliers not to be prepared to put products on the market at the lower prices so that there will be a shortage of a particular product.

Only at the equilibrium area of balance, only at the compromise price where buyers are prepared to buy and sellers are prepared to sell - only here will the product clear the shelves and exactly meet the demand with no shortages or surpluses.

Imbalances

The implications for the business manager are that imbalances in supply or demand often occur in practice and all such imbalances give an opportunity for someone to profit.

For example, where there are surpluses someone may be able to buy in bulk cheaply even at below the equilibrium point if the seller gets desperate and panics. Then the business manager can sell later or somewhere else at a profit.

Similarly, if there are shortages, the business manager may be able to buy in bulk from a little known source or produce more efficiently, or import more cheaply, in order to sell at a profit to eager buyers. Such opportunities only exist, of course, because markets and information like human beings are often imperfect.

As long as markets are not in equilibrium there is the possibility that the business manager can take his profit by using new ideas (methods, inventories, substitutions, arbitrage, importing and exporting, etc.) to get products more cheaply than others and sell them at prices that others cannot match.

Special Information

Profits can be made all the way to the equilibrium point - which is perhaps never quite reached except in theory due to the complexity of the real marketplace. In short, if the business manager is smart enough or determined or well-informed in terms of innovations, there is always a profit to be made.

> **If the business manager is well informed, it is likely that there will always be a profit to be made.**

In terms of basic economic theory - the equilibrium is where the shelves are clear in the store - all the goods have been sold - there are no surpluses and no one is asking for the goods - no one that is, who is prepared to pay a dollar or even a penny more than the equilibrium price. No shortage, no surplus.

Now, in practice, there is virtually always either a surplus or a shortage so that equilibrium is rarely ever reached. It represents a theoretical point only. In real life there is always room for an innovative creative business manager with new ideas on how to beat the established competition.

PART II
MONEY

Inflation
Inflation and the Marketplace
Growth of Money

Old Saying:
- Greed -
The love of money is
the root of all evil

CHAPTER SIX

INFLATION

Supply, Demand and Money

Money is like any other commodity, apples or oranges or gold or corn.

> ## MONEY
> **If there is too much of it - its value will go down ↓**
> **If there is not enough of it - its value will go up ↑**

When the value of money goes down, money will buy less – less of anything (goods, services, labor – skilled or unskilled).

When money generally buys less over a period of time we have inflation. This is just a form of words that says "the cost of living (i.e., just about anything) has gone up, has become greater, blown up or inflated."

> ## INFLATION
> **When money generally buys less over a**
> **long period of time, this is inflation**

What Causes Inflation?

Since inflation is a general rise in the level of prices, it follows that only governments can cause inflation.

Inflation

Individual producers can only produce shortages or oversupply of their own goods or services. Only governments are big enough to increase the supply of money to the extent that it results in inflation. Governments do this in four ways:

1. by printing money and giving it to government employees and businesses in return for goods and services,
2. by introducing bylaws, taxes and tariffs that reduce the supply of products relative to the money in circulation,
3. by issuing bonds and paying out interest on these bonds over different periods of time.
4. by setting the interest rates charged by the central bank for commercial loans.

Setting these interest rates has the effect of increasing or decreasing the total amount of money in circulation. Therefore, the tendency of governments is to repay their debts in inflated money.

DEBT

Low interest rates result in many businesses borrowing unnecessarily. This creates a situation that is like a herd of wild donkeys – there is little scope for skilled horsemanship but it can trample down anything in its path.

Wars

Additionally, governments cause inflation by going to war, which is highly inflationary.

War disrupts the supply of food, clothing, appliances and other necessities which then increase in price due to shortages. In addition, war causes more money to be printed, which then compounds the problem of more money and fewer goods. This is not to suggest that war should always be avoided. Obviously, wars must exist in the interests of law and order. However, we must understand the full economic implications of war when it cannot be avoided.

Prohibitions

Governments also cause inflation by enforcing prohibitions of certain goods such as alcohol, guns for self-protection and recreational drugs. These goods then become products on a black market at greatly inflated prices.

The general taxpayer also pays out more in taxes because of the expense of policing the crimes of mugging and burglary since these crimes are often associated with people requiring the money to purchase these banned products.

All these payments by the taxpayer greatly increase the amount of money in circulation relative to the number of legitimate goods and services available - in other words, more inflation.

However, necessary spending on pensions or security cannot be inflationary in themselves, since such spending is a valid cost of production.

Pensions are to encourage productivity as an end reward for labor. A fairly high level of incomes and pensions is also necessary to create markets for goods and services.

> **If people do not have money they cannot spend it.**

Government Spending

Spending on security is necessary to protect and defend the storage and selling of products. The question is, How much of such spending is needed?

All government spending is inflationary other than what is necessary for the continuation of orderly and progressive business and social life. How many government programs pass this test?

The implications of inflation or expected inflation for public goodwill are profound.

Coming inflation will increase the value of real property, commodities, stable currencies and, perhaps temporarily, more traditional hedges like gold or silver.

Also, assets bought on borrowed money generally become more valuable as the debt is repaid with inflated and less valuable money.

Losers under inflation are:

- Fixed incomes
- Savings in cash or near cash
- Bonds (unless indexed to inflation).

These become generally less valuable as the value of money decreases.

Inflation is to money, what cancer is to the body. Since most transactions are carried out in money, inflation has destroyed many economies.

> **Governments cause inflation**
> **by waging war,**
> **charging duties and taxes on goods,**
> **enacting prohibitions**
> **and creating shortages in general.**

What Causes Deflation?

The opposite of inflation is deflation. This occurs when money becomes more valuable due to its decreasing supply.

When there is not enough money in circulation for people to buy what they need, money increases in value and therefore prices tend to go down so that sellers can attract the smaller amount of money available.

This can be true generally as in the Great Depression or locally in places where money is scarce where second-hand items, including gold, can often be bought more cheaply.

Once again the laws of supply and demand will work – less money in circulation leads to money becoming more valuable.

> **DEFLATION**
> **When money becomes more valuable**
> **due to its decreasing supply**

Inflation is related to the problem of shortages and oversupplies.

> **Deflation occurs when prices**
> **generally remain lower for a long period of time.**

CHAPTER SEVEN
INFLATION AND THE MARKETPLACE

Inflation is certainly caused by too much money chasing too few goods but what, in turn, causes this imbalance to occur?

An Overheated Economy?

Some believe that the economy can become overheated by over-activity and that this over-activity gives rise to full employment which in turn causes too much money to get into circulation thus leading to inflation.

This might be so when the economy produces unnecessary goods like bombs, submarines, bureaucracy, spies and eyes on the people to maintain control - like spy helicopters, bugs and so on - but in this case (and it certainly is the case at times in virtually all modern countries worldwide) it is governments that are causing the inflation not the marketplace.

The overheated economy is a myth perpetuated by media morons who have forgotten that people's buying and selling is the basis of all economies.

In fact, only governments can cause inflation and conversely, it is impossible for the marketplace to cause sustained and general price rises.

Oversupplies

The marketplace only responds to demand and if it miscalculates and overproduces by mistake (which it certainly does at times), this overproduction cannot be inflationary since it will cause prices to fall.

Remember what happened to the price of oranges when the produce shelves were stacked high with them? The price of oranges went down ↓ - not up.

What happened to potatoes or cabbages when the farmers produced too many? The price went down ↓.

What happened to the price of digital watches or strawberries when they were a glut on the market? Price went down ↓.

But what happened to the price of imported strawberries when they were out of season and were few and far between? The price went up ↑ .

So, overproduction cannot cause inflation, rather it is underproduction that will cause inflation.

Shortages

Shortages caused by tariffs on cheap foreign imports to protect home products will cause prices to go up.

In summary, the laws of supply and demand are unrepealable.

When supplies goes up - prices go down,
→ this is not inflationary.

It is when supplies go down,
when shortages occur, that prices go up,
→ this is inflationary.

It is shortages, not oversupply,
→ that causes inflation.

The business manager, therefore, needs to know that mass production of any good will lower its price and conversely underproduction of any good will raise its price at least temporarily until the higher profit margin attracts competitors into the market.

Underproduction, not overproduction is inflationary and the overheated economy is a myth.

CHAPTER EIGHT
GROWTH OF MONEY

Another problem in the marketplace, the behavior of money, is not as simple as that of other commodities. The ways in which it varies, its peculiarities, will now be looked at in more detail.

Behavioral Theory of Money

> **Money is worth what people think it is worth**
> **- no more or no less -**

In theory a government or even a company could print as much money as it wished provided people had faith in the stability of its value.

In practice some governments are almost an example of this since they produce money largely to the extent that it is acceptable to people throughout the world.

When people begin to lose faith in any major currency, such as dollars, euros or pounds - its value will fall.

This may be due to:

1. too few goods being available for the money issued, or
2. lack of faith in the future production of goods and services, or
3. fears that the world economy and/or civilization will soon perish in war, or
4. fears that the world's economies will succumb to internal crime or corruption.

Therefore, when people lose faith in the major currencies, the whole structure crumbles - the Titan Falls.

Public Support

In theory too, public advertising could help support to a great extent the value of any currency. Though this has rarely been used.

Appeals such as "Be a Patriot" or "Protect the Value of your Savings and Earnings" might well prove to have as much of a stabilizing effect as credit or tax manipulation.

The Government Money Wheel

A government money wheel can be thought of as governments spending and income where governments take in taxes and borrows (or prints) money, then sends the money out by way of spending and handouts and wages and pensions to government employees and suppliers. This money then enters the economy by way of spending and investing through banks and stocks and bonds and brokers and businessmen.

The Multiplier

As the money enters the economy it reproduces its effect by passing from one spender to another so that the civil servant or pensioner buys groceries and the supermarket gives money to its employees. The employees spend money on purchasing food, shelter, entertainment, transportation and clothing.

As money percolates through these various layers, it gradually dries up in terms of immediate circulation as some of it, at each level, is taken out of direct use by way of savings.

However, even the savings, for the most part, eventually find their way back into circulation as they are invested by banks and lent out to homeowners, purchasers of cars, home improvers, buyers of appliances and small businesses.

This percolating of money through the economic system is known as the multiplier effect. The multiplier effect will vary greatly with wages and prices from one region to another but is usually about a multiple of four or five.

The Multiplier and Political Decisions

The multiplier effect is not often taken into consideration when political decisions are made.

For instance, when deciding what will be the effect of building new homes in a district, it should be understood that the multiplier effect will increase the number of supermarkets, estate agents, accountants, house repairers and other small businesses. The increase in the number of such businesses will promote competition and thus lower prices.

It follows that the decision to build or not to build is the decision whether to automatically increase the number of new jobs and the availability and competitiveness of virtually all goods, foods and services.

THE MULTIPLIER EFFECT
Is where money multiplies itself as it percolates
through successive layers of spending.

The Entrepreneurial Boomerang
What Goes Around Comes Around - Investment

Investment in business starts off as the savings of private individuals. From there it passes to business, often through banks, as investment. Business uses this investment as capital to produce goods and services, paying out wages and salaries to individuals who in turn buy the goods and services produced.

This cycle or circular flow proves that what goes around comes around in the sense that the various parts of the economy are interdependent.

**If business pays low wages –
people will not have the money
to buy goods and services
and if people do not save,
or do not have enough money to save,
then business will not receive enough investment
to expand or even to sustain itself
in the face of hard times.**

Business needs profits to create jobs but to create profits it must have land, labor and capital.

The multiplier effect of the jobs created will build up the entire economy.

The law should allow business to have land use and permissions to operate and workers should be prepared to work for whatever the business can afford (subject, of course, to a minimum wage).

Those who work should save and those who control the savings should be willing to support the business manager's new ventures.

Everyone must take chances for the economy to grow, create jobs and more and better products for more people at lower prices. Enlightened self interest, as the people take a long-term view of their own welfare, will send out better things to others and others will send back better things to the people.

In short, the business manager is a key part of the boomerang - what goes around comes around.

> **BOOMERANG**
> **Is the part of the circular flow that sends products back to the spender**

Many Complex Factors

It will be fairly clear by now that for business management to succeed either by starting off new businesses or by introducing new ideas into established business and thus fight off competition and lethargy, many complex factors must come together in a unique and synergistic way.

Often this does not happen with the result that the mix of workers, savers, investment bankers, spenders, venture capitalists, civil servants, professionals, politicians and entrepreneurs just do not come together in the right way.

This is hardly surprising when we consider that millions of economic building bricks are swirling around daily in the great globe of the world economy. The result is that a chart of national economic activity goes up and down in a totally unpredictable way and in fact looks like a drunken snake.

Economic Troughs

The implications for business is that it should try to buy and invest in the troughs of economic activity and sell or otherwise realize profits from its investments (produce, lease, lend, etc.) at the peak of the snake's back. Again, the classic role of the business manager but in this case it is like arbitrage over time rather than over places or markets.

Buy at the trough, sell at the peak and take the profit that comes between the key times - this is the business manager's mandate.

PART III
MARKETS

Markets
The Sapling Forest
Pyramid of Profits

Money grows on trees.

The entrepreneur is a tree.

In the same way,
business growth is a tree.

CHAPTER NINE
MARKETS

Different Markets

The established markets may have convinced governments to protect them with licensing, zoning, planning permission, health-based restrictions or tariff walls of steel. Let us just note that each of these situations will create a different market.

Other factors such as climate, fashion, laws, culture, general health, religion - almost any factor except price and quantity - creates a totally different economic environment.

That is to say, a different market where the buying and selling behavior will be different. Where, in fact, more or less will be sold or supplied than in other markets.

For example, less ice cream will be sold or demanded in the winter and more in the summer. A seller might find that only 5 or 10 gallons of ice cream per day will be sold or demanded in 40°farenheit, whereas at the hotter 90°farenheit, 60 or more gallons will sell in a day and, of course, the cheaper the ice cream the more will be sold at any temperature.

> **The lower the price the more will be sold and demanded in any market.**

Supply and the Market

The relationship between supply and the market is similar to the relationship between demand and the market. Almost any factor other than price or quantity will create a whole different market with respect to supply, as noted above. The entrepreneurial manager should consider these relationships and check out logical explanations for the various behaviors.

The opportunities for profit in all markets: food, money, bonds, stocks, commodities, land, houses, machinery, information, etc., will then be more clearly understood. All are subject to the same basic tendencies (or laws) of supply and demand.

The difference in price of the same product in different markets is fundamental to the business manager's opportunity to buy in a cheap market and sell in a high-priced market. This form of entrepreneurship is called arbitrage (as discussed in Chapter Three) and can best be understood by looking first at the supply and demand of money.

CHAPTER TEN
THE SAPLING FOREST

Business Risk

The business manager or entrepreneur who takes risks and organizes a profit on a consistent basis is the human form of the essential synergy of business. In other words, the human hand of business risk.

Risk or loss must be paid for with the possibility of profit. Otherwise, no one would risk their all on the cost of sales. These costs include not only the basic product or service but also, for example, security officers, cleaners, sales persons and distributors.

Therefore, the business manager must be the master of risk which is the essence of business. The entrepreneur must be lucky or have special knowledge, having which is a form of luck anyway.

Of course, the landowner or the laborer or the capital provider could also become the business manager but the business manager's role is separate. It is the role of the entrepreneur who creates a new firm or socioeconomic entity.

Economic Growth

Economic growth can only be encouraged from the bottom up.

The benefits of top down growth, if any, are few, small and far between. This is because small-growth upwards cannot easily be diverted out of the mainstream of the economy whereas large capital is like water flowing downwards. It cannot stay suspended at or near the top of the growth tree. Trees cannot grow downwards.

Economic growth can only grow upwards, that way it has few avenues of escape to either side as small business cannot easily liquidate or expatriate or afford to be wasteful.

Avoid Leakages

When politicians or community leaders or businesses and boards of directors are given large sums of money, leakages may occur. There is not only a temptation but a very clear and open opportunity to divert these funds into private accounts or in return for kickbacks to ineffective business sideshows.

Cash Aid

Cash additions are like fertilizer. The only place for fertilizer is in the ground, around the trees where it will cause the trees to flourish and grow.

Growth needs to be worked into the soil preferably from basic natural resources such as mining, logging, farming, drilling for oil and water and gas. Then it is turned into jewelry, bark pictures, paintings, woodcrafts, furniture, ornaments, seaweed, pills, cans of fish and food and other things needed for survival. This will include self-defense, social advancement and law and order - such as guns, traps, bait, fishing tackle, schools, tents, homes, roads, boats.

**Economic handouts at higher levels
(from governments, charities or foundations)
will tend to be stolen by intermediaries
and often will not reach those who need it the most.**

Small Growth Upwards

An entrepreneur is a tree. Plant a whole bunch of entrepreneurs and soon you will have a forest of growth and food and health.

Trees must grow from the bottom, from the soil up. However, trees often take time to grow but on the other hand, in the right soil they can grow quite quickly.

So entrepreneurship cannot spring from the big boys downwards in a hurry as it were. Rather, entrepreneurship must grow from the little acorns and seedlings and twigs; from the small business owners upwards - farmers, handcrafters, computer programmers, printers, writers, gardeners, dressmakers, shopkeepers, repairers, builders, carpenters, professionals and educational publishers. These and many like them can become big biz if given the right economic soil. Prosperity grows from the little sticks upwards.

In brief, nothing grows from the top down.
All good things spring up from the sea or the soil.

Historical Precedent

This kind of bottom-up development took place throughout economic history with the development of colonies through shipping trade (arbitrage) and agricultural growth. This lead upwards to cars and books and computers and banks and bourses (stock exchanges) and traders and ships and on upwards and up and up into universities and scientific research institutes.

This pattern continues as wealth grows upwards into the ever finer point of the pyramid of economic growth.

This growth-up theory holds that wealth grows upwards and does not trickle down, generally, as many modern economists have mistakenly believed.

> **Growth-upwards Theory holds that wealth grows upwards and does not trickle downwards to any great extent.**

The Up-Down Theories

Concepts such as capital grants are eventually trickle-down theorems as is the idea of isolated venture capitalism, tax breaks and many other up-down methods of economic development.

Up-down theorems do work in certain narrow circumstances but not in general.

For example, it may work where the wealth can trickle through somewhat freely where there are no opportunities for bribery or backhanders.

However, where the downward flow is restricted by siphoning off at higher levels "up-down" will work only to a limited extent, if at all.

Indeed, in theory, up-down must nearly always fail as it may have no lower levels of wealthy and well-off and comfortable consumers to support it.   The lower levels of wealth are needed.

Growth of Wealth

Wealth starts where natural and basic products start.   Where farm produce, fish, handicrafts, clothes, building supplies, mining and quarrying products, precious metals, silk, cotton, gems and so on are collected, gathered and produced.   Then they are protected from becoming waste, molded and packaged. Finally, they are shipped by small producers who then use their profits to buy goods from retail stores.

These small firm owners then use their salaries and profits to buy luxury products such as cars, houses, swimming pools, holiday homes and boats. These producers and sellers then save and invest through venture capitalism and investment in stocks with all the imperfections noted above.

The important point is that the cycle (unless it is broken by government confiscation or mafia greed) begins at the bottom - not at the top. Wealth begins on the farms, on fishing boats, in mines.

It should be institutionalized in the farmers' markets where there is permitted only produce and artifacts and clothes made by the stallholders.

The tree's trunk is the beginning of wealth and small retail is the thick layer of branches. Large and luxury retail is the third level of thinner branches.

The top layer of small branches and leaves is the canopy of luxury big ticket items that forms a protective shade. These will protect the trees from winds and suns of the economic cycle.

Wealth begins in the basic farmers' markets. However, before trees will grow at all there are a fair number of environmental conditions that must be met.

Growth-Upwards Theory of Money

All economic laws - whether at county, state, province, country, nation or federal union level, must provide for development from the ground-up if the economic infrastructure is not to run the risk of collapsing at some point in the future.

In summary, injection of capital at higher levels, such as bonds and financial investments, runs the risk of being siphoned off, stolen, hidden, to save it from creditors and put into minimally productive investment.

Indeed, these leakages are bound to occur unless the lower sections of the socioeconomic-pyramid are in place to hold up the higher levels.

**The growth-upwards theory
can therefore be summarized as –
entrepreneurs make profits in lower levels
then spend the money in developing higher markets.**

CHAPTER ELEVEN
PYRAMID OF PROFITS

In graphic form, economic growth flows upwards as shown in the following diagram:

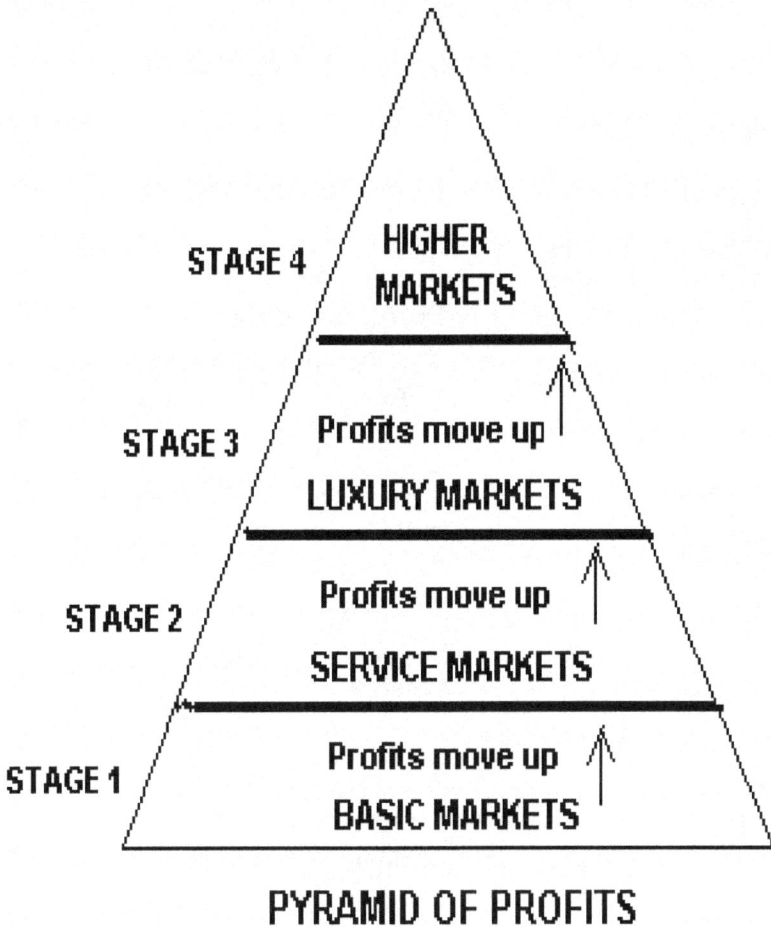

STAGE 4 — HIGHER MARKETS

STAGE 3 — Profits move up — LUXURY MARKETS

STAGE 2 — Profits move up — SERVICE MARKETS

STAGE 1 — Profits move up — BASIC MARKETS

PYRAMID OF PROFITS

This could also be shown as a cycle or a continuum but will be simplified into the following four sets of market:

STAGE 4

HIGHER MARKETS
Investments in Commodities, Ships, Armies, Stock Exchange, Insurances, Equities, Interest-bearing Bonds, Loans, Banks, Currency Dealing

STAGE 3 - ↑
Profits move up
to Higher Markets

LUXURY MARKETS
Homes, Factories, Buildings, Bridges, Roads, Mass Productions, Large Farms, Yachts, High Fashion, Prescription Drugs and Jewels

STAGE 2 - ↑
Profits move up to
Luxury Markets

SERVICE MARKETS
Some Retail and Services Industries, Appliances, Fine Clothes, Household Goods, Cars, Hotels, Small Boats, Leisure Products

STAGE 1 - ↑
Profits from these
move up to
Service Markets

BASIC MARKET
Moving and Structuring of Basic Foods and Earth Products, Poverty Banks, Basic Clothes, Handicrafts

Basic Market

A basic market is where there is sold only artifacts made by the stallholder or food produced by the stallholder.

Therefore, furniture, painting, sculpture or jewelry made by the stallholder can be displayed or sold but not such an item made by someone else. Food grown and packaged by the stallholder is permitted but not prepackaged food from any other source.

Among the mainstays of basic markets are small open stalls or closed booths for merchandise. The use of arbitrage, e.g., moving food from farm or sea and selling it in small amounts, preservation by drying, purifying, cleaning, icing (or fridge), canning and similar packaging, as well as lapidary and other artistic services, furniture and craft-making, fabric making and selling.

Therefore, economic growth is based on the bottom line business manager - the marketeer or booth owner, the open table crier. So, those who buy from farmers or fisheries or miners or quarries are not entrepreneurs until they go to some trouble to sell to the public on a consistent basis - thereby creating a firm.

Purpose of Basic Market

The idea is to cut out the mass producer of any kind and avoid all the ecological costs, such as pesticides, chemicals, additives that go with mass production.   These are best left to the second level of markets.

If the stall or booth-holder does add unhealthy ingredients then this information should be clearly marked on the label or displayed with a large sign to the buying public. This information would probably make the item less competitive so that the system tends to bias the market towards organic or near organic clean produce.

By selling original works only, the basic market encourages mainly poor farmers, producers, artisans or artists.

This is the purpose of the basic market - to self-lift the poor out of poverty by building a wide and deep foundational layer of economic self-sustenance for the poor or marginal or landless or land renting. All this is to support the entire economy of the region with a broad base for the economic-pyramid.

The Middle-Level Markets

The Basic Market leads to the development of corner stores, very small general stores, small restaurants, small garages, well-trained artisans, repair shops, organized craftsmen which represent the next step up from the basic market.

The basic market helps form lower levels of Phase Two which leads on to larger retail goods and service establishments. And so the sapling forest grows upwards.

The Higher–Level Market

The top level, even the middle levels of this pyramid, cannot exist unsupported in mid-air. Therefore it makes no sense to try to stimulate business at a higher level until there is full support for that level at all the lower levels. That is why many third world countries are in a state of collapse even after large sums of money have been thrown at their higher levels.

In weak markets these higher levels lack the support of profits and high standard of living growing upwards from owners, managers and workers at the middle and lower levels.

In such weak markets there are not enough consumers with money at the lower level to support the higher level.

Support for Basic Markets

Instead of giving money to level one small industry, money has been thrown at politicians and big business firms and institutions before society has the up-growing funds and customers to support these higher institutions.

The poor first, then the small business classes should have been the sequence of economic aid. These in turn would have created and built up and supported the middle level institutions.

It follows that it should never be necessary or desirable to support or initiate higher level institutions. These institutions should grow up spontaneously, in such a way and in such a sequence and in such places, as to serve the natural needs of the economic levels below them.

Trees cannot be grown from the tops downwards. The entrepreneur is a tree of economic growth and must grow from the soil of natural resources upwards.

The middle and lower levels must be put in place if the top of the pyramid is to succeed in trickling down any wealth. In short, wealth must grow upwards before any of it can trickle down.

The historical development of all the more prosperous economies have followed the economic pyramid model. For example, Western Europe, North America, Australia, New Zealand and South America all followed the Stage One through Four phases of economic development.

Top-Down Support

Top-Down support is more often Topple-Down support as was the case with India, most of Africa, Central and South America.

Top-Down Revolution

Most of Asia all had the pyramid shattered by top-down revolution. This led to rule by capitalists and the creation of large masses of unemployed and impoverished peasants which have failed, for lack of cash in hand, to support Phases 2 - 4 of economic development. This dashed all hopes of a trickle-down invigoration of the economy.

Large masses of unemployed poor are not only a human but an economic tragedy. These poor should all be employed moving, clearing, artifacting, subdividing, packaging and selling natural resources in order to support themselves.

Neither Loans nor Handouts

These impoverished people need neither loans that they cannot repay nor handouts to make them dependent on exploiting capitalist enterprises. They need education and training and organization into small, one and two and a few person businesses to extract and use the natural resources of the sea and land which are available freely or at low cost.

> **Handouts to the poor create only a culture of dependency and unemployment and beggarism.**

When the middle and lower level markets have been built up, then, at this stage, the market structure is ready for political support and encouragement by way of laws and rights in a structured business-friendly environment.

Some of the more important political rights and legal frameworks will be discussed in later chapters.

> **There are four levels of markets – Basic, Service, Luxury and Higher.**

PART IV
BUSINESS PLANNING

Business Predictions
Conditions for Growth
Business Rights and Conditions

Stats NOT Math
Statistics –
the science of approximations
should be the guide,
NOT mathematics
which is an exact science

~

The best laid schemes of mice
and men gang aft agley
(Rabbie Burns)

CHAPTER TWELVE
BUSINESS PREDICTIONS

The business manager needs to know if there will be a return on investment. If so, when?

The Fourth Factor

In fact, the true entrepreneur or business manager needs both brilliance and luck to succeed. This is why the entrepreneur has been dropped as the fourth factor of production by many modern economists.

The business manager cannot be described by a number. Modern economics has become a largely mathematical science. It ever seeks the exact answer by following econometric models. It is impossible to factor into these models events such as:

- genius
- unexplained success or failure
- luck
- future interest rates
- probabilities of success
- events outside normal control such as weather or labor unrest

Non-Predictable Models

It is not possible to set up a model that successfully predicts. That is why models that are designed to predict, do not work.

Modern economists tend to dream up numbers that are supposed to reflect these events. However, such numbers have no firm basis in fact and are pure speculation. They may be based on undependable past records.

So, say the economists, let us just ignore the entrepreneur/business manager and let us just say that there are only three factors of production - all of which we can quantify - land, labor (skilled and unskilled but routine) and capital. Great, they say, now we can have nice clean math models to predict everything.

Of course, most econometric models predict absolutely nothing. They are even less accurate than astrology.

Indeed, econometricians are the modern astrologers who use numbers to try to predict the unpredictable. Whether they are more accurate than mere chance is the subject of much statistical analysis and academic discussion.

Economic activity is so complex with so many millions of people and currency units, commodities, services, decisions and products swirling around in the great globe of buying and selling. No math model could possibly predict even the most basic result with any degree of consistency.

Anyone who could make a model that would consistently predict the movement of even, say, the Dow Jones Index could take over the world's wealth in a month. Nobody is about to do this. There is no model that can predict Gloom to Boom or even Boom to Doom.

Model Fanatics

Why do people continue to pay good money for models that do not work? Economy or Astrology? Several reasons.

In most cases they are not spending their own money:

- it's their firms' money,
- their bosses' money,
- their investors' money,
- their readers' money,
- their shareholders' money, or
- their taxpayers' money.

So who cares? Again, it's a confidence trick designed to safeguard and raise salaries, the magical black box that raises them above the level of the ignorant masses whose only function is to pay out monies to an exotic elite.

Another reason is that the econometric model has acquired the status of a cultural icon. Who would dare to attack a sacred icon of our times? Why, only a business manager of course and now this entrepreneur has become of no importance because they have been demoted alongside St. Christopher and St. George to the ranks of non-persons or so, at least, many of our modern economists, the latter day astrologers, are trying to tell us.

Blame the Model

The final true but unadmitted reason for the use of the math model is that it is a useful alibi for bad decisions.

If things go wrong - blame the model.

- *Why, that's the best model known to science.*
- *I went by the model. If it didn't work, well I've done the best I could.*
- *Why did I make that dopey, half-witted decision? Well, I followed Dr. Astrologer's Econometric Model which, of course, while not perfect, is wrongly believed to be better than*

mere chance and therefore the best to be found.
- *I just follow state of the art science. That's why I bombed-out so badly.*
- *I blame the Econometric Modeler.*

Statistics not Math

The truth is that only entrepreneurs can make economic events happen. Mathematical predictive models cannot quantify the work of the business manager.

These predictive models should be abandoned in favor of a more general socioeconomic approach. This will produce rough guidelines. Statistical tests that do work rather than precise answers which are entirely wrong in most cases, being based on unknowable and unguessable trends.

Accountants often say
It's better to be about right than exactly wrong

Let us be clear that math may be just fine for other more specialized aspects of economics but it is not right for predictions. This is simply to argue in favor of the science of approximations - statistics - rather than math -

with respect to business growth.

Math - the supposed science of exact answers - is simply not the right way to measure general economic activity in all its immeasurable complexities.

The Best Factor of Production

In fact, not only is entrepreneurship the fourth factor of production, it is the most important of the four factors. It is the fourth factor that provides the synergy for the other three factors to work together - land, labor and capital - to produce anything at all. Without entrepreneurs, economic production would be nil, zero, zilch for all its land, labor and capital.

Under labor we include all routine, learned skills from top administration to manual level but the business manager is more than just a worker. He is the synergist who adds up 3 + 3 and gets 7 which is a very lucky number.

How then should the entrepreneur plan ahead for business projects? What exactly are the conditions needed to facilitate the growth of business?

Complex as is the whole process of growth and success, there are a few economic principles that are known and at least about as much agreed upon as anything else in economics. For growth to occur there are, in fact, about fifteen circumstances that must be present and these will now be discussed in the next chapter.

CHAPTER THIRTEEN
CONDITIONS FOR GROWTH

Economic growth takes place from the soil, rivers and the sea. Just as the rain falls and the sun shines down to cause the fields and waters to produce life growing upwards, so capital is sown into the fertile field of the economy. Business growth soon flourishes and springs up to provide great wealth in many varied forms.

The whole process of entrepreneurial growth and success is complex, nevertheless, there are a few simple economic principles that are accepted. These may be summarized not only in the four factors of production for growth and sustaining the economy but also in the fifteen laws of economic development as follows:

Fifteen Conditions Favorable to Entrepreneurship

1. **The Limited Company** - no one wishes to risk all on a business venture. No share owner should be personally responsible for the debts of the company.

2. **Laws of Debt Recovery** - so that even small firms should get paid what is owed to them. For example, automatic return to rightful owner of all monies or goods stolen or garnishee orders by courts to banks or employers requiring them to hand over regular amounts from non-paying debtors to creditors.

3. **Right to Do Business** - without government permission. Government permissions, local, state or federal are often given only to political insiders. Such permissions should be more freely available.

4. **Lower Taxes** - people will work harder if they can keep more of their own money.

5. **Freedom of Labor** - free rights of skilled labor to enter and leave the country and move freely within the economy.

6. **No Restrictions on Closure** - such restrictions were conceived to protect labor from layoffs but act only as a disincentive for entrepreneurs to hire labor in the first place. Laws or edicts cannot hold back the tide as King Canute discovered.

7. **Law and Order** - the rule of law keeps down predators such as robbers, thieves, extortioners, blackmailers, false advertisers, burglars, confidence tricksters and embezzlers. Business needs security for customers to walk the streets.

8. **Freedom to Move Capital** - capital goods and currency need to move in and out of any country or region. Entrepreneurs or established business will not send capital in, if they know that they cannot take it out later.

9. **Good Educational Systems** - good workers must have technical skills, literacy and be computer-savvy as well as being well in advance of the three Rs – Reading, Writing and Arithmetic.

10. **Good Wages for All** - people must be well paid in order to create markets for goods. Also they will be more productive if they are healthy and happy, being able to afford a balanced diet, healthy homes and outdoor recreation.

11. **Fair Civil Laws** - No economic region or country can afford a populist court which penalizes business in favor of the populace. Awards of damages should be compensatory and realistic not punitive. Punishment should be the preserve of criminal courts. Losers in court cases should pay all legal costs of the winner but not necessarily other expenses such as research, expert witnesses and other discretionary expenses. Punitive damages drive small businesses out of the jurisdiction. Fair laws should be the criterion.

12. **Free and Good Communications** - Internet, phone, fax, mail, TV, cable and broadcast radio and print should all be free of government control or ownership.

13. **Good Transit Systems** - Canals, roads, rivers, seaways, rail, air, tunnels fit for trains, cable cars, cars, trucks, boats, barges, cargo planes, trains, buses, bicycles and taxis.

14. **Mass Spread of Investments** - good investments set up by governments or firms should be widely available - even in a small

way in order to get almost all people on board the money ship. For example, new public offerings of shares should be lotteried off, in part, to small savers to get commitment from the people as customers and workers. Small savers must take more chances than large investors and therefore are more entrepreneurial.

15. **Interest rates** should be fair to savers as well as to borrowers since savings are in part used by banks to lend needed capital to entrepreneurs who create jobs. This is why low interest rates can never rebuild depressed economies. Personal savings should be built up so that savers can start up small businesses.

There are several problems with low interest rates that make them an all-round bad policy.

They may:
- drive much-needed capital out of the country
- encourage unnecessary or frivolous over-borrowing
- drive some firms into bankruptcy

- encourage almost anyone to bid for house prices that are too high, so causing a bubble in property prices, especially if there is a shortage of houses.

Additionally, cheaper exported goods being sold in a dumped and depressed currency will not necessarily sell much more abroad if sold under the stigma of near bankruptcy.

MAXIM: *The Business Manager's Golden Rule*
Only those laws should be passed that are necessary for orderly and progressive business to take place.

Business needs - Fewer and Fairer Laws

CHAPTER FOURTEEN
BUSINESS RIGHTS AND CONDITIONS
Which Rights or Conditions?

Many entrepreneurs have great ideas that might well succeed but for government rules that prevent outsiders from becoming insiders. Governments acting on behalf of entrenched private interests are the main obstacle to entrepreneurship and the creation of more jobs.

A business manager should ask, Which rights or conditions do I really need for this project? Research should then be carried out to enable the business manager to choose the best nation or province that comes closest to providing a healthy framework for the business.

Some of these conditions may provoke controversies and encourage fresh thinking, research and questions among would-be business owners and students of business.

For example, irrespective of our personal choice as to climate, culture, creed or color, what countries are most conducive to real innovative management and entrepreneurial outreaches? Ideally, these answers should help the practical, innovative manager to redirect creative ideas to unexpected places and opportunities.

Libertarian Conditions

Briefly, there are some 49 basic legal conditions which will help free market operations, the exact number depending on precisely how these rights are defined.

These libertarian conditions may be said to be socio-economic legal rights within which entrepreneurship can flourish. Without these, the business manager may well find restraints on normal business activities, thereby constricting the growth of jobs and prosperity.

Of course, conditions for business are rarely, if ever, ideal and successful business management always calls for perseverance in the face of adversity.

However, there are important conditions that the business owner needs to look out for in the country of choice. Not all of these conditions are always needed but many of the freedoms or rights to be outlined are necessary to engage in successful business.

The reader should bear in mind that this book in general presents only a brief synopsis of just what the business manager really needs; an outline that will help to guide the worldwide business manager to the most hospitable climes for the practice of business professionalism.

These basic rights or conditions either provide opportunities for new business or, if they are absent, restrict new business ideas.

Just what the business manager really needs depends on what rights are granted to citizens in a written constitution.

Laws are set by constitutional standards and both old and new laws are permitted, controlled, modified or rejected by any country's written constitution or bill of rights.

These set the limits for even elected government on the well-accepted principle that no one and nothing is above the law - not even the legislature that passes the law or the judiciary that reviews it or the administration that carries out the law.

A Model Bill of Business Rights?

Here we present for the business manager a model bill of rights, a partial draft constitution that might well serve the business owner as a legal infrastructure or underpinning, a statement of needs in terms of political economy and a passport. These basic business freedoms are just what business managers need to travel. The structure of this passport consists of seven sets of rights each within seven groups of conditions and choices.

The seven different kinds of rights or freedoms, each with seven subsections, are moral, security, political, financial, social, judicial and personal. All 49 rights are important for economic development.

Fewer and Fairer Laws

The 50th freedom should be the right to possess such a passport. It follows that this Right #50 should be the right to a written constitution restricting what governments can or cannot do to the business world and therefore the 50th freedom may be viewed as the right to live under fewer and better laws.

This floating 50th right underpins all the other 49 conditions listed here as needed to a greater or lesser extent by business in general and by the business owner in particular.

The 49 rights or conditions for a political economy of business ownership will now be looked at in greater detail.

These rights or conditions would lead towards the free market development of more and better jobs, income, wealth and a higher standard of living for all through cheaper goods and services.

**Business must be built on a foundation
of rights and legal opportunities.**

**For business managers – governments are
Public Enemy Number One**

PART V
THE BUSINESS
LEGAL FRAMEWORK

Business can only flourish within a framework that enables the entrepreneur or business manager to act in a consistent manner. An essential part of a business-friendly environment are the rights of the business owner.

    1 – Moral Rights
    2 – Security Rights
    3 – Political Rights
    4 – Financial Rights
    5 – Social Rights
    6 – Judicial Rights
    7 – Personal Rights

Actual Event

In early 2011, a young man in Tunisia was prevented by government rules from becoming a self-employed fruit seller. He burned himself to death. Mass protests against governments soon followed.

Six months later the Arab Spring uprising had set free, for the first steps in democratic business, all of Tunisia, Egypt and Libya.

CHAPTER FIFTEEN
MORAL RIGHTS

There are many business decisions that involve freedom of the press, free speech, freedom to protest, religion, dress codes and fairness in the allocation of jobs. In a word – moral rights.

These economic issues are not confined to publishing and newspaper businesses but relate to a wide variety of business situations. The entrepreneur or business manager may have to confront such questions as:

- *What can I legally sell – when and where?*
- *Are there any age limits for customers of my products/services, e.g., videos, tobacco or liquor?*
- *What can I legally say or comment on?*
- *What can I legally print or advertise?*
- *What dress code can I require for my employees?*
- *What can I legally research/keep in my records?*
- *What religious holidays will need to be observed for my employees, customers or trading area?*
- *Can I be sure that government inspectors are properly qualified to carry out inspections in my field of business?*

The specific conditions relevant to moral rights will now be looked at in detail.

1 - Free Speech

This is the most fundamental of all human rights and covers the freedom to speak the truth as one knows it.

Freedom of speech is primarily the right of everyone to speak or write, without restriction, about their beliefs or interpretations and include some of the following:

- the right to have opinions about private or public figures and their ideas and plans,
- the right to support political or other causes in oral or printed or recorded form,
- the right to reveal hidden plans, terms or agendas.

Free speech may therefore involve the revelation of fraud, lies, deceit or deception.

Also permitted under free speech is the interpretation of religious, political, classical or popular writing and art. No literary law should be used to victimize any religious or ethnic minority.

Historical facts tend to be distorted by the hindsight of ideology. Therefore, there should not be any official version of history propagated by governments. No one should be victimized because they refuse to accept an official version of history.

Truth

Truth - the proof that a statement is factual, or that it is a sincere opinion based on the known facts, should be a complete answer and justification against all charges of libel or slander. This should hold whether such knowledge is deemed to be in the public interest or not.

Truth, and the right to speak it, is an absolute freedom that either exists or does not. It cannot be frittered away in shades and doubts; it does not lend itself to ifs ands or buts.

2 - Free Press

Freedom of the press is the institutional form of free speech. It includes all the rights under free speech but applies to all the media, not only to reporting of the news but to expressing opinions and ideas and criticisms.

This right may also indirectly provide protection of copyright for pictures, photos, designs, blueprints, maps and other graphics.

But above all, freedom of the press is the right not to be censored by either governments or private interests. That is to say, the right not to be banned or suppressed.

This right applies not only to printed books but also to talking books, recordings, journals, disks, tapes, news, internet, telephone, TV, radio, audio, video, films, artworks or word displays such as those in the sky or on clothing or buildings.

To ensure freedom of the press there should be no government control, monitoring or ownership of any media.

All media outlets should be independently company-owned or reader/worker cooperatives or privately-owned with a cooperative element. Some media at least should always be owned and based in the home country or home federation of countries.

There should be no list of restricted press or publishers and no record kept of book buyers or library book borrowers. These are police-state tactics and amount to censorship.

On the contrary, a free press should include the right to read. Although publishers may well have lists of customers, these lists should not be sold or made available to governments for censorship purposes.

The freedom of the press should be absolute in all matters of truth, so that truth should never be censored even if presented in fictional, parablic or other creative form. Opinion should never be censored if it is acknowledged as such.

3 – Right to Walk

The right to walk in protest includes the right to petition, demonstrate, assemble and engage in peaceable confrontation.

Those who rule have a responsibility to give an account to the ruled. They should not be permitted to hide from the people whose lives they are restricting.

When rulers hide, they can see themselves as benefactors. Even though in reality they may be surrounded by sycophants heaping praise upon them.

The ruled should have a right, in peace and good order, to walk in front of their masters in protest and to dispel the myth that the ruler is a popular helper and hero.

4 – Right to Know or Hear the Truth

This freedom is the right to receive correct information regarding health, safety, society, crime, politics, science or history. This is the counterpart of the right of a free press and includes the right to hear the truth in consumer advertising, job offers and descriptions and to know how tax money is being spent.

In regions where there are many poorly educated voters, there may be a leadership of the moron for the halfwit by the numbskull. Business may be at risk of discretionary mismanagement in such places.

Minimally, citizens should have the right to know what is safe to eat on such matters as organic, refined, bleached, synthetic, hydrolyzed, genetically modified, transfats, radiated or other altered states of food.

The right to truth also includes:
- receiving unbiased, fair and accurate news reports
- knowing what are the real threats to society
- the reasons for taking all action on behalf of citizens
- knowing why a nation goes to war
- the right not to be given false information

Citizens need to know what others say they know about them. Every citizen should have a right of access to all personal information held about them by any public agency such as governments, their agencies, schools, colleges or police forces.

They should also have a right to access, e.g., to receive a complete copy of, information held about them by private bodies who might make such information available to third parties like employers, schools, credit or loan officers, mortgage or insurance or other businesses.

Everyone should have a right to know what others know - or think they know - about them in order for mistakes to be corrected and so that both sides of the story can be told. This will enable lawful business to be carried out without the sabotage of falsehood.

> **There are two sides to every story and both sides need to be told in the interests of fairness.**

5 - Religion

Freedom of religion is the right to practice any religious belief or to belong to any religious organization and should include secret or underground religions.

The right to practice a religion includes the right not to be forced to support, by way of taxation or subscription or fees or otherwise, any religion or philosophical group other than one's own. This means the complete separation of church and government at local, regional or central level.

Personal relations, including employment or marriage, should not be subject to any constraint upon the religious, philosophical or political beliefs of either party as a condition of that relationship.

No taxpayer's money should be used to support any religious belief. This should apply irrespective of how good the church, the religion or social work being done. If a religious organization is doing such a good job as it often claims in countries where it sticks its hand out for handouts, then let it be supported by voluntary contributions from its own adherents.

The state should be impartial and use taxpayers money only to support secular state business and employees. It is irrelevant if a religious organization can do the job cheapest or even best.

> **Separation of church and state financially is of the very essence of religious freedom.**

6 - Effective Public Spending

This right calls for a fair and effective disbursement of all contracts and public monies at all three levels of government.

The civil service or administration should not support favorites, privileged persons or firms. Privileged oligopolies (ownership by a small number of people) should not be issued with licenses in the public's name.

Public monies should not be given away to foreign governments in emergencies except for needs to be met only in kind. This includes food, medicines, tents, huts, water, clothes, rescue work, fuel, small arms and other necessities of life.

Gifts of credit, cash, heavy arms or loans or any other gifts to foreign governments or their public sector institutions usually finds its way into the hands of thieves masquerading as:

- advisers
- consultants
- administrators
- politicians

- intermediaries and similar fronts

This applies to both the country of origin, that is the donor and the country of final destination of any aid.

7 - Meritocracy

Taxpayer-Supported Jobs

All taxpayer-supported jobs (e.g., policing, hospitals, teaching) should be given to those who have taken written examinations which have been objective, anonymous and accredited. Such jobs should be allocated only on the basis of degrees, certifications, diplomas and those with the highest level of qualification should receive priority.

Ideally, where more than one person is fully qualified for a position, the job should be shared serially on a term limited basis of no more than two years in any one position.

The theory that it is possible to be overqualified for a job is untenable and a mere tool of discretionary power which surely must involve corruption. It is also a violation of a citizen's right to do government work in a field of trained expertise.

Therefore, the principle of meritocracy requires that individuals have a right to at least a minimum wage-level public job on the same grounds as others. This would lead to a recognition of their real qualifications on a rotating two-year basis.

> **Nothing can disrupt an economy more than unqualified employees.**

Elected Officials

Where possible, all major public jobs should be filled by referendum. That is, the vote of those whose tax money pays the salary of, e.g., fire chief, police chief, hospital manager, school principal, college president.

Such middle-level public jobs should be elected every two years. No one should be eligible to hold any public office, elected or appointed, for more than five terms of two years. These rules would reflect the more widespread availability of educational programs in modern times.

No More Nepotism

The old system of jobs for life grew up in days when only the privileged few went to college or were considered fit to rule for reasons of family privilege.

Those who have been given jobs on the basis of political, social or family connections - after the fashion of the dark ages - are unlikely to allocate jobs to underlings on a purely meritorious basis.

Likewise, their appointed sycophants will also be afraid of appointing those who are better qualified than themselves. The end result would be incompetence and stupidity permeating the whole public system from top to bottom.

```
Arbitrary rule and incompetence
trickles down.
```

Discretionary Power

Discretionary power and arbitrary rule is morally wrong. It could well result in an unjust downward cycle that might end in anarchy or widespread poverty. Here the business manager would have little part to play.

Even in the short-term, discretionary rule may well result in bribery, corruption and bad decision-making which fails to distribute scarce resources on a fair basis or to the best use. In this way, an economy based on privilege is strangled by a counterproductive allocation of money and monies worth to the least productive persons.

In such a world, parasites might well prosper while hardworking professionals such as business managers may struggle to stay alive.

The only libertarian way to reverse these plunges towards anarchy would be to gradually demolish the welfare state with its discretionary handouts and to replace it with a meritocratic state where hard work and entrepreneurship is rewarded.

At present, in too many parts of the world, bureaucrats with life tenure who cannot be fired, year after year eat up the foods and goods of the people. The taxpayer including business owners are being doubly robbed.

In the first place, by being unable to get a government job for which they are often better qualified than the incumbent parasites.

In the second place, they are robbed by having to pay for the entrenched incompetents not to mention suffering under parasitic mismanagement.

No to Exclusive Licenses

Life for small business can be a hard struggle against those privileged to obtain licenses, permissions or basic rights.

Therefore, there should be no exclusive licenses issued by governments for either recreational (e.g., liquor, gambling) purposes or for providing essential services (e.g., medical, prisons, schools, childcare). Opening up these areas to business managers would make many more jobs available on a more competitive, efficient meritocratic basis.

Recognition for Education

No one should be denied the chance to work at their highest level of expertise in a recognized trade, profession or occupation. Competition lowers the cost of all goods and services.

Legislators should make the final decision as to what is or is not recognized training in a bona fide field. This decision should be made primarily on the basis of return for investment over an extended period of time for the benefit of gross national product.

What the business manager needs is a culture of public respect for higher education. This is often lacking in some parts of the world today. Ideally, only persons with good advanced degrees should be given high-level jobs or permitted to practice.

Experience is useless if it is based on inferior or even merely basic qualifications. It needs to be recognized that a bachelor's degree is seldom enough to justify such jobs as a university or college lecturer, a scientist in either the social or natural sciences, a mid-level or higher civil or local government official, a CEO or a professional.

Higher degrees sometimes known as masters, professional certifications or doctorates should always be required for such jobs - especially when employed by the public (i.e., taxpayer-supported) sector.

Unqualified persons with only basic professional qualifications, if any, and lower level degrees are often given jobs virtually in secret. They are often protected by a firewall of secrecy in public office to hide the perverted culture of fear against those who are highly qualified in their fields.

Taxpayer-funded jobs in the complex modern world should no longer be left to mere discretionary allocation.

When the present system was developed, people understood their place in society as lower, middle or upper-class and a rough meritocracy worked on unwritten rules.

Therefore, all jobs that are supported by the taxpayer should be:

1. open to scrutiny,
2. given to the best qualified in terms both of examinations and professional experience,
3. rotated on a 2-year incumbency basis,
4. not paid excessive pensions.

The practice of careers for life, at taxpayers' expense, has been outdated since education became universal.

Qualifications

All high-level professional jobs require three things:

1. a mastery of a body of knowledge by degrees, diplomas and certifications
2. relevant experience in the field by the passage of time in performance – this is what you get if you don't drop dead.

3. special aptitude for creative innovation in the job by published speeches or articles, awards, books, copyrights, patents and inventions.

Know Your Rights

Citizens need to know exactly what rights they have, if any. Do they, or do they not, have the freedom of living in a meritocracy or are they condemned to live in a welfare system which promotes a state of dependence on handouts and doles which are all largely discretionary? Doles are merely miserable bribes to persuade the masses not to rebel. Such persons have little money with which to do business.

A meritocracy could bring not only justice, but opportunities for the able, higher living standards, greater law and order through creative management and entrepreneurship. Meritocracy often leads to innovations and new ideas which open up many new opportunities for the business manager.

> **Business professionals need relevant experience, ability to make creative innovations and mastery of a body of knowledge.**

CHAPTER SIXTEEN
SECURITY RIGHTS

Business needs to operate within a framework of security and predictability. Therefore, many business decisions may arise such as the following:

- *Is the business property legally available?*
- *Can the employees operate safely and securely?*
- *Is there adequate security in the area? For instance - policing, fire control or waste disposal.*
- *Does the trading area have any restrictions with regard to age, race, color or creed?*

1 - Auditing of Public Purse

This is the right to have public spending audited. Spending of the taxpayer's money needs to be subjected to proper accounting standards and audited by an accountant.

To ensure a balance of practice and theory, ideally, the accountant should have both a license in public auditing and a fully accredited AACSB masters degree in accounting. They should also be professionally independent and not employed by the entities to be audited.

Public inspectorates should have authority over all philanthropic organizations which receive tax relief. They should also inspect firms that deal with:

- foods
- civil service
- housing
- safety of business premises and products
- police
- highways
- colleges
- schools
- healthcare facilities
- parks
- orphanages

Charities should also be subject to inspection. This would ensure that contributions from the public are used directly and solely for their designated purposes, not on other activities, even if related or contributory. Contributions from the public should be for specific purposes.

For this reason, a government inspectorate should embrace the whole of public funds accountability. This includes all non-taxpaying, non-profit organizations operating within the jurisdiction of all three levels of government. These should be regularly audited for detecting all forms of nepotism, jobs for friends, contracts for contacts, fees for family kickbacks and bribes in general.

Anti-Corruption

There should be a strict code of ethics for all those who receive public funds whether elected, appointed or contractual.

This code should set out rigorous criterions for conflict of interest. This would ensure that those who profit directly or indirectly from public funds would be prevented from giving benefits to those who have contributed to their family, political party, organization, close friends, partners or other associates.

Such unauthorized benefits should be invalidated and set aside permanently, to be garnished and put back in the public purse by the judiciary.

Fair Accounting

In the interests of disclosing and avoiding fraud, all limited companies and corporations should also be audited on a regular basis by auditors who should be full-time employees of the people (i.e., the state).

A full public accountability and disclosure should be required for the following:

1. tax breaks for corporations
2. limited liability
3. press releases, true or untrue
4. government jobs being offered to the public from time to time
5. the raising of capital for publicly traded corporations

Property Notaries

It is recommended that the business manager should consider buying real estate property in those countries, such as France, which ensure the appointment of state employed lawyers known as property notaries. These notaries work in all areas and towns to monitor leases and sales of real property.

This scheme is to make sure that both parties, buyer and seller, understand what rights and privileges are being sold or rented. This is to serve the purpose of fairness and legality in the disclosure of all the relevant facts. It is also to facilitate the transfer of all leases and contracts for the sale of property and to register and monitor all aspects of property deals - other than the price which, of course, remains a matter for private agreement.

This is in contrast to hiring private adversarial lawyers to represent the buyer as opposed to the seller. Such a system is an outdated, pointless form of legal warfare that benefits no one but the party who may be the greatest fraud. A referee is needed.

2 - Law and Order

This is the right to codes of criminal and business law. This includes a local gendarmerie, special volunteer police and investigative agencies at all three levels of government - local, state or central.

Each central government needs to have the exclusive right to coin and print money. Governments at all three levels should have to define and punish crimes and keep the peace with an armed police force but not to make any retroactive or ex post facto laws.

Civil law which borders on criminal investigative agencies should also check on such business problems as theft, false advertising, fraud, false pretences, embezzlement and failure to pay monies due.

Sentences for crimes should be based on:
1. reimbursement
2. deterrence
3. rehabilitation
4. punishment

A balance of all four of these elements is needed to clean up crime for the benefit of business. Law and order is needed for citizens to go about their daily business.

3 - Liberty and Life

This is the right to go freely about one's business without interference, to be free of slavery and forced labor, whether one is in prison or at large.

It is necessary for every business manager to be free to search for new business opportunities or ideas and to go about personal activities without interference or hindrance.

Habeas corpus is the right to be released from prison when a judge or court decides that the imprisonment is unlawful.

The right to a secure life is the right of all to be free of assassination or murder.

No citizen should be stopped or questioned by the police, army, civil service or other authorities unless the detaining officer is aware of probable cause. The arresting officer should be aware of good and sound legally accepted grounds for suspecting that the person being stopped has probably committed a crime.

The right to personal freedom should pertain until the free citizen has been convicted by a jury of a crime warranting incarceration.

In theory, the right of liberty would also include the freedom to practice one's legal trade or profession anywhere in the world, either at home or abroad. In practice this right does not exist.

4 - Peace

This is the right of all citizens to enjoy quiet and peaceable existence in pursuit of their trade, profession or personal recreation. The right to go about one's business freely and peacefully is fundamental. Therefore, all steps should be taken to maintain the peace.

As mentioned in an earlier chapter, war is inflationary and though profitable for some, such as armament makers, war is unprofitable for business in general.

To discourage vested interests from promoting war, expenditure on equipping and maintaining the armed services should be limited. Many businesses have perished because of the sudden outbreak of phony hostilities and the business manager must look with favor upon those countries that have avoided civil or international wars in recent times.

5 - Privacy

There should be no invasion of privacy. Governments are the elected representatives of the people and should not spy on those whose interests they represent. People should be entitled to hold any peaceful opinion. Therefore, it should not normally be necessary to maintain any special branch or political police. If people's opinions do stray from the peaceful then any probable cause of future or past crime may certainly be investigated by court order. But the business manager needs stability and privacy not police-state interference.

6 - Integration

There should be equal opportunity for persons of all colors and creeds in public education, public employment and in the allocation of all government contracts.

This requires that there should be no discrimination because of creed, color, age or gender in public places of work and leisure, including the places where people live. Everyone should have the right to live in integrated housing, as opposed to ghettos.

Everyone should have the right not to be threatened in public places. No ghettos should be permitted to build up or to continue since their very existence precludes free enterprise and entrepreneurship.

In countries where ghettos already exist, governments should encourage integrated housing on a nationwide basis. This could be achieved by means of orderly and fair cash compensation for those who wish to move. This would be repaid by the existence of more business opportunities. Everyone should have the right to relocate, with compensation, to a ghetto-free area in order to avoid the real or theoretical threats of ghettos.

There should be a right to live and to do business in a mixed and integrated community.

7 - Personal Protection

This is the right not to be tortured. Furthermore, to be free from undue punishment from the police or other government officers.

This freedom also covers brutal assaults on a citizen's person, religion, property or home and covers the protection of business premises, papers, effects, goods or chattels from search and seizure.

There should also be a right to self-defense, of citizen's arrest of trespassers and the authority to use all necessary restraint to hold intruders who invade private property.

People should be allowed to control their financial affairs as they wish by paying in cash or checks and by avoiding debt and credit cards.

Finally, it is important to be able to set up business companies with liability limited to the amount of capital put into the company in the first place.

Business can only be carried out within a framework of safety and security.

CHAPTER SEVENTEEN
POLITICAL RIGHTS

An orderly political framework is essential for the successful operation of any business.

- *Are there any restrictions on the citizenship of potential employees?*
- *Will all the employees enjoy fair voting rights?*
- *Will government contracts be fairly allocated?*
- *Will the business manager be able to fire failed employees?*
- *Can a system of checks and balances be applied to the business?*

1 - Citizenship

Every legal resident should have the right to claim citizenship. In an ideal world, citizenship should be owned and should belong to each citizen as an asset which may be exchanged for another foreign citizenship.

For example, in cold but affluent countries there are many retired persons with the means of self-support. They often do not have the right to go to warm and poorer countries as investors or entrepreneurs.

In many poor but warm countries there are young, able-bodied, ambitious but unemployed professionals and artisans who have no money and therefore no opportunities to practice. If these two groups were to exchange citizenship, both individuals and both countries would benefit.

This exchange of citizenships, if it were introduced, would build towards an eventual citizenship of the world. Citizenship exchange would bring sunlight to rich old bones and opportunity to strong young minds - money to poor countries and workers to affluent countries.

Even a lower-level reciprocity of rights of visitation and residence would encourage extended visits to affluent countries. This would aid the educated poor in search of work. It would also facilitate those with a little money to seek small business opportunities in poorer countries. Reciprocity of travel and immigration rights, as between rich and poor nations, would

1. spread wealth more equally among citizens of both deprived and affluent nations,

2. relieve governments of the tendency to hand out the taxpayer's money to foreign corrupt leaders on a backhander basis and

3. generally democratize business opportunity.

It follows that all rights to pensions, education, residence, loans, financial and social security, healthcare, travel and similar rights should be reciprocal and equal for citizens of all countries concerned.   Ideally, welfare handouts should be phased out.   In summary, all this would result in a fairly full reciprocity in immigration and citizenship.

All rights of foreign nationals to emigrate to wealthy countries should be based on reciprocal rights of affluent citizens to emigrate to the sun.

These reciprocal rights should be inclusive of all relevant rights and apply to jobs for both men and women. This should include the right to enter the professions, attend college or university, the right to own land and enter business.

In the absence of such a reciprocal agreement, the tendency to-day is to encourage loans to poor people in undeveloped countries. These loans come from banks specializing in advances of short-term money and from small venture capitalists. This seems a less effective way to encourage small business since it places a burden of debt on the shoulders of the new entrepreneur.

2 - Checks and Balances

Business managers often have to lobby politicians for the provision of goods or services. Almost anything is likely to be purchased by governments and the business manager needs to look for a system of voting that is reasonably predictable in order to achieve sales.

It is important to be able to choose a political candidate whose ideas regarding regulations and laws conform, as near as possible, to the aspirations of the business. Balanced government helps to ensure fair shares of contracts and jobs.

3 - Three Levels of Democracy

The economies of most nations seem to work best with three tiers of government. Where there are only one or two tiers of government, economic development rarely takes place.

Primitive societies with one small group of king, elders and witch doctors tend to provide an opportunity for greed on the part of just a few families, perhaps sharing a very little power and income with their enforcers and supporters.

> **Checks and balances are needed for business economics to work effectively.**

In a large economy, only two tiers of government would mean that persons in small communities seeking justice and equity must appeal directly to central government. This usually makes it impossible for small voices to be heard.

For instance, having only two tiers of government may mean that the right of judicial appeal is at the discretion of the courts. Additionally, it could create huge backlogs of unheard lawsuits and appeals.

At least three tiers of democratic government, whether executive, legislative or judicial, is needed for the following reason. There are often revisions, appeals and scrutiny of the innumerable injustices, frauds, crimes, bribes and nepotisms which inevitably occur in free enterprise societies.

The middle tier of regional government, variously known as state, provincial or country, needs to be sufficiently autonomous and powerful to act as an effective buffer between local (county, parish, municipal, etc.) and central or federal government.

A middle tier of government is usually based on a shared historical cultural identity. In some cases, these could be formerly separate nations now federally united under a common language. It might be under common economic interests preserving and improving traditional, cultural and trade identities and loyalties.

To be effective, such provinces need to be free states. That is, autonomous and self-perpetuating with the right to exist, raise taxes, self-police and use such funds as the middle-level government needs.

Therefore, central government may be responsible for such aspects of interstate macroeconomics as:

- public health
- law enforcement
- transportation
- immigration
- defense
- federal appeals courts
- international affairs or
- communications

In other words, to be workable, a regional tier of government should not be merely a local talking shop. It should not be subservient to central government and therefore become susceptible to being closed down.

Indeed, it is important that all three levels of government should have the strength and self-propagation in order to dispense stability for entrepreneurship at all levels.

In this way the higher tier of government overcomes the tendencies of the lower tier to misallocate scarce resources such as jobs, contracts, court or jury-awarded damages in favor of the local interests which rarely serve the wider economic well-being.

Remember –
Democracy is the Rule of the Rabble.
Weak democratic governments can be
particularly harmful to business.

---

4 - Fair Voting

The allocation of government contracts for roads, utilities, communications and teaching skills needs to be carried out in a fair and democratic way. This includes fairness in the growth and fair spread of money and monies worth.

> **Everyone who pays taxes in a nation should have the right to vote on the principle of no taxation without representation.**

5 - Direct Choice of Leaders

Preferably, steps need to be taken to prevent narrow vested interests from achieving a controlling power through government.

The leaders of all three branches of government (legislative, judicial and executive) and at all three tiers of government (local, regional and national) should be elected by fair vote, every two years within the term limit of five terms.

6 - A Fair Press

Places of learning are also media. There are two sides to every story and the press (print, screen or spoken) should be required to give both sides of every business, political, personal, religious or social controversy.

In print or classroom or internet this should include, at least, a brief but fair statement of the opposing point of view.

Equal Time

However, in TV or radio, which have a much more direct and immediate impact on the mind of the viewer or listener, there is a more formal need for equal time to be allocated to all major controversies.

In order to give further balance to content, all media should be privately owned and not subject to government control.

7 - Recall of Failures

To get a job, many candidates present claims which are often misleading, if not false, selective or exaggerated. While it is easy to prove false pretenses in cases of outright fraud and lies, it is often impossible to get rid of the shadowy claimants who may prove to be failures.

Irrespective of the validity of non-binding promises and aspirations, it should be possible for an employer to fire any employee from CEO to laborer for failing to meet expected high standards in any job.

Failures, per se, should be dismissable without any compensation, including pensions. These terms should be clearly stated in any contract.

This right to the recall of failures would encourage and attract capital in its various forms. Also, voters would be more inclined to vote and entrepreneurs would be more inclined to delegate and hire if they enjoyed the absolute right to fire where necessary.

> **There are always two sides to every argument – that is why some media should be required to give equal time for all major controversies.**

CHAPTER EIGHTEEN
FINANCIAL RIGHTS

Financial questions will arise concerning wages, loans, interest rates, government red tape and movement of capital in and out of an area.

- *What is the current minimum wage, if any?*
- *What is the government policy on pensions?*
- *Will there be freedom to choose a company name?*
- *Are there any government restrictions on location, hiring and firing?*
- *What about redundancy payments?*
- *Will the business be responsible for any taxes?*

1 - Good Wages

It is a false economy on the part of a business to pay its employees and distributors as little as possible. In this mode there is little incentive to succeed on the part of those who should be helping the business to achieve its goals.

However, paying out higher wages or commission than any competitors could lead to bankruptcy in the long-run.

Yet in theory, as wages continue at a reasonably high level, people as customers will have the money to buy new goods and services. In this way, the entrepreneur can always be on the lookout for new ventures or expansions.

A Fair Minimum Wage

A partial solution to this problem of high wages causing bankruptcy is for the laws of the land to come to the rescue of business. This should be done by introducing a fairly high minimum wage which all businesses would have to meet. This would prevent employers from undercutting each other with respect to wages.

A higher minimum wage, quite apart from any deductions for tax, etc., would stabilize the reasonably content minimum wage workforce. This would also create basic markets and the widespread ability for customers to pay for many other goods and services.

Merit-Based Pay

In addition, to increase productivity and further boost domestic markets and jobs, any of the following systems of merit-based pay could be adopted:
- bonuses
- commission

- equity sharing
- share options
- piecework

Any of these should be in addition to a legal minimum wage. Such ideas, while not being mandated by government, could be allowed some tax-relief. Firms using these incentives could be taxed at somewhat less than the regular tax rate.

Workfare

If a government undertook to be an employer of last resort, this could help to eliminate the elaborate system of dependency on public support and welfare.

This could be done by paying a fair wage to the otherwise unemployed for public works on any of the following:
- property repairs
- roads
- railways
- waterways
- canals
- and other transits

In some western countries this is known as WORKFARE and is to be welcomed as building up the infrastructure for the benefit of business owners, customers, suppliers and servicers.

The business manager could save a lot of money, time and effort by moving to a region where there has been plenty of training for both full-time and part-time skills. There, in an atmosphere of self-drive and initiative, the local government should have provided a structured environment that will help to create jobs. This would be a win-win-win situation for the employee, the employer and the government tax collection department.

2 - Free Business Entry

This is the right to do business in any of the following ways:

- buying or selling in cash, in credit or in kind, one's goods and services
- setting up a company with limited liability
- free of licenses
- free of competition from oligopolies
- free of competition from any government-controlled monopolies

This is, in fact, the freedom to enter any business without unreasonable restraint.

Right to a Name

The most basic element here is the right to describe one's business in simple words. Business owners should be able to choose any name except where fraudulent intent can be established in a court of law. This right is not to be taken for granted and in fact is not given in all major western countries. Its importance cannot be overestimated as a symbolic sign of business freedom.

Right to Start a Business

Anyone should be able to start any business, profession or trade at any time, subject only to anti-fraud prevention measures.

In the case of professional groups, degrees and certifications should be displayed in public view such as:

- on doors
- mail addresses
- letterheads
- cards
- advertising
- videos
- internet
- spoken on audios

This should be made clear at all points at which business is carried out with customers, owners, lenders, media, suppliers, servicers, employees or advisors.

Let the client or customer decide with whom to do business. Closed shops should be closed down. (When governments or unions forbid a firm to do business – this is known as a Closed Shop.)

Closed shops should be closed down.

Right to Use of Property

The businessperson should be able to use any property for any business, subject only to area-wide zoning for groups of businesses.

Right to Rational Zoning

Planning permission, so-called, in some regions is not just for planning. It is operating permission. It is permission - period. It is the right to exist.

The business manager should know that the right to do business does not exist in all nations, so that such places of pitfall can be avoided in advance. Rather, the business manager should gravitate to those regions where people are given their economic freedom as much as possible.

Decisions as to what business is needed should be made by the business manager in the first place and in the second place by the customer. Such decisions should not be made by any civil servant or other bureaucrat.

The government, as a matter of principle, should hold no long-term business interest since all for-profit business interests should be the property of individual investors.

All business areas should be zoned and not be subject to individual planning permission from government. This means that occupiers of business property in each zone are free to carry out business in the named groups, without any further government permission. This, of course, is always subject to inspection of safety and security standards. Examples of zones are:

- retail
- light crafts
- offices
- residential (including retirement)
- holiday
- hotel

- entertainment
- schools and education
- heavy industrial/scrap
- engineering
- manufacturing
- farming

These enterprise zones always create jobs and wealth as well as taxes.

Also, all citizens with less than half a dozen employees or assistants should have the right to run a small business from home on phone or internet.

Tax Breaks

Ideally, the government should encourage entrepreneurship through education at all levels from primary to Ph.D. This should be carried out by way of practical, formal coursework and training in all fields.

Another encouragement would be by advising and granting a two-year tax-free status to all new start-up limited corporations (limited companies) of less than 200,000 net worth, employing less than six persons.

In the case of shared ownership, each equity owner should be entitled to benefit from only one such company in whole or in part. This would exclude re-incorporations of substantially the same assets as previously exempted.

Qualified private firms and individuals should be free to offer supplementary services in all fields on a competitive for-profit basis.

No Exclusive Licenses

This is easily taken care of by not issuing exclusive licenses to anyone.

All trades, occupations and professions should be open to all qualified persons. For the sake of impartiality, qualifications should be issued by a representative public body, e.g., schools, colleges and universities - not by the trade or profession itself.

It should be considered illegal to profess to have a qualification unless issued by such an objective body.

In short, no monopolies (ownership by one person) or oligopolies (ownership by a few persons) should be licensed or protected by government. This includes giving licenses such as moneylending, pawnbroking, medicines, credit granting, gambling, liquor, insurances and similar sources of government permissions.

The business manager needs, as much as possible, free competition in the interests of the consumer.

Natural monopolies such as railways, waterways, tap water supplies, should be controlled, rather than owned, by government in the form of voluntary juries, boards and commissions.

Participative Management

All owners and managers should be required to have in place a formal structure to hear about the problems, ideas and suggestions of their workforce. Likewise, there should be a right to part ownership.

All firms with 200 or more permanent employees should provide a fair equity savings ownership plan (ESOP) for workers. This would transfer at least a 20% equity stake to employees within a 20-year period.

All citizens should have a right to set up a co-operative. These could be organized by either workers or customers. Laws and regulations should be encouraged which set up and advise wholly or part-owned co-operatives.

Government or state-employed auditors should be appointed to protect creditors and shareholders. This would help to ensure honesty and fairness for all business.

3 - A Market Economy

The business manager needs to know that governments are often the worst enemy of business.

All levels of government can easily be influenced by legal campaign and party contributions. The purpose of these inducements is often to protect local or large vested interests and in short - to keep out the outsider.

The entrepreneur is the ultimate outsider who needs the freedom to move capital internally or outside the country in order to benefit from arbitrage or to start new ventures. The right to a free market economy should be a legal right, not a mere hope or aspiration.

Libraries of books have been written on this topic but the present commentary may help the would-be business manager to get at least some feeling for the rights under this freedom.

Small Savings Critical Mass

First of all, the business manager or entrepreneur is not the main provider of capital and is not a capitalist at all in the same way as venture capital firms, banks, savings and loans and financiers.

However, the entrepreneur often needs to have some capital to start off a viable business from a garage or home office or other small premises. That is why Small Savings Critical Mass (SSCM) is so important and needs to be achieved and maintained by the entrepreneur. This is to the entrepreneur what seed is to the farmer.

It is important from the point of view of economic development that small savings should be encouraged and helped to grow to the level of critical mass. That is to say, the level where the saver can reasonably expect to enter a good, small business with success or can even live modestly on basic interest payments. This level is normally in or around 400,000 per family. This of course is well known to many governments who seek immigrants. It is roughly the amount they require of immigrants to ensure their near self-sufficiency.

Using a system of meritocracy and help in kind would not give rise to parasitism and manipulation like the present fiasco known as the welfare state.

Savings spread thinly among many people is rarely lent out to support new ventures. Rather, if lent at all, it should go to those with secure incomes. This of course precludes the business manager in most cases.

Small savings in the hands of individuals are good for starting a business.

High Interest Rates

Governments should be in favor of as high a savings rate as possible to encourage new business startups.

Small capital should be available in a form accessible to entrepreneurs and practical small business. It should not be dissipated across the entire economy as it often is in many third-world countries where there is a rich/poor dichotomy. Unless more economically savvy governments take over, many economies will collapse.

Savers should be able to escape from their Small Savings Poverty Traps and a strong middle class developed that would be allowed to create jobs and economic growth.

It is a far-fetched notion that civil servants should be thrifty or even stingy with the public purse. Rather, there should be an attitude of free enterprise. Public servants should look for good investments in return for public expenditure, no matter how high the initial outlay. Thriftiness is worse than useless, in itself, unless it can be converted into investments that show a fair return.

The driving motivation of governments should be to invest, to build up and to sustain Small Savings Critical Mass (SSCM) among the populace.

When companies are put out of business by non-entrepreneurial government decisions, employees of such companies become public charges. So also do their families and associates and all those whom the government might well have saved from unemployment.

In short, the economic multiplier is working in reverse in a downward spiral. All those affected are driven downwards into a negative and increasingly wide vortex of failure and impoverishment.

On the other hand, when small business is given the right government help, such as planning permission or high interest rates on savings, small business drives into an upwards-positive spiral. There is then no need for the taxpayer to support, out of the public purse, the family and employees of the business owner.

4 - Effective Taxes

Taxes should be fair and as low as possible. They should be spent only in the interests of the commonwealth and audited by independent accountants.

Business managers have a right to know what becomes of their hard-earned money handed over to various levels of government. Is it achieving the purposes for which it is intended - to enable citizens to lead a full life in peace and good order?

Therefore, the main question regarding taxes is - not how much but do they achieve their purpose? Do they work?

- Is the taxpayer getting value for money?
- Is there an orderly society?
- Is there any assurance that contracts will be kept?

- Is there a fair and level playing field for all business?
- Is there any assurance that money owed will be paid?
- Is there the rule of law?
- Is there really guaranteed social justice or merely the rule of the ambulance chaser?
- Are there reasonable employment laws?
- Public health?
- War only against those who threaten us?
- Honest supervision of all financial management and accounting (and for that matter marketing)?
- Is there safety in all products and in all transit?

The list of what government should do with taxpayers' monies is almost endless. The bottom line is - Does the business manager feel that business is getting a fair crack of the whip in return for its tax handouts?

Beware of Extra Charges

The business owner should be wary of extra charges and hidden stealth taxes which can, more often than not, be budget busting.

For example, all those who pay local government tax should have an absolute right to basic safety, hygiene and trash (including hard and metal and electronic garbage) removal services on a regular basis without any additional charge. Otherwise trash removal charges can be enormous.

Taxes should be collected fairly across the board and not extracted unfairly from any one group. A local income tax is far preferable to a land, property, house or spending tax.

Spending tax (VAT) is grossly inflationary and has proven disastrous to those nations imposing it.

There should be no billeting or poll tax - not even for war. The rule is - if you can't afford war, don't fight. If you can't beat them join them - in peace. The day of the nation state is gone - states are now provinces. International alliances are the superstates of the future.

No savings, investments or other assets should ever be confiscated on the pretext of unproven guilt or mere suspicion.

Other than contraband goods themselves, no assets should ever be confiscated by governments until after due process of law through the criminal court system.

One Rate of Tax?

Preferably, one rate of tax should cover all health services for all citizens. There should also be a national minimum pension for all citizens beyond working age.

In business, one rate of corporate income tax should cover all obligations of the employer to employees. This would aid business in the planning, administering and paying of a set predictable amount of payments to government.

5 - Balanced Interest Rates

Some business owners who borrow money wish to keep interest rates low but this is not necessarily the best thing for their business. It may be better for them if interest rates were much higher and they did not borrow at all. It might be better for them to wait until they had a really good product to sell, resulting in bigger profits that would more than cover the higher interest rate.

To borrow at low rates may be a credit trap that could ruin the business in terms of credit, credit rating, bankruptcy or worst of all, in terms of reputation.

The Problem of Interest Rates

The problem of interest rates is a complex one - not a simple matter of optimization. Some economists teach that low interest rates will lower the price and increase the sales of exports - 'ceteris paribus'. This means - all other things being equal. However, in the real world nothing is ever 'ceteris paribus'.

What is true in economic theory is rarely true for the real world of business. It is often better to wait for a truly profitable product, irrespective of interest rates.

Don't Forget Savers

The important thing for business is that an interest rate exists that is fair to savers and potential entrepreneurs, as well as to borrowers.

> **If savers are driven to save or to spend abroad then the nation or province or local community with the lower interest rates may find itself short of capital to lend to entrepreneurs.**

There is a point of balance (or equilibrium) that maximizes both savings and borrowings by small business and entrepreneurs.

This equilibrium point should be found and maintained by trial and error but will certainly vary within market, economic, social and cultural needs. It is the point at which a healthy growth rate of jobs and taxes is being maintained.

6 - Receive Debts Owed

All contracts voluntarily entered into and properly witnessed should be enforced by direct garnishee court orders. That is, funds should be directly debited from the accounts, credit cards or by liens on the property of those who owe the money. These funds should be transferred to the accounts of those who are owed. Those who are owed should not have to undertake lengthy lawsuits to get their rightful possessions.

It should not be necessary for the courts to make orders for repayments, restitutions or debts and then impose fines and further court orders. This circus not only keeps lawyers in years of profitable earnings but encourages thieves to swindle and evade in the sure knowledge that they will keep most of their ill-gotten gains.

Modern technology can keep track of owed monies paid to the close friends or relatives of non-payers or swindlers and such monies or assets can easily be electronically confiscated and returned to the victims.

Some countries now have laws enabling government to confiscate assets from those whom they suspect of helping so-called terrorists. However, they have no such laws enabling the victims of proven bad debts or other rip-offs or wrongdoings to receive their own property back. This could be done automatically by court order and without having to bring expensive lawsuits. Suing a non-payer is often like trying to arrest the Devil (a futile exercise and a joke).

Fully qualified accountants should be appointed by the courts to supervise the garnishment of all monies owed.

7 - Fair Shares for All

The way to help the poor of the world is not by handouts, doles or welfare payments. How then are the poor to be helped? This should be by means of helping them to become self-sufficient. This is not just a matter of charity but a matter of building up viable markets for the entrepreneur's goods and services.

- payments in kind (e.g., clothes, food, water)
- paying out for garden land or small savings critical mass (SSCM) amounts,
- poverty banks giving out equipment such as water distillers, sewing machines, gardening tools, manual water pumps, handymen's and builder's and artisan's equipment.
- training and education at all levels by mandating all large companies to set up ESOPs, Equity Sharing Ownership Plans (employees stock),
- introducing workers to the practice of participative management,
- making common land for small-scale mining, seashore, even seaweed gathering rights available to all,
- encouraging new small entrepreneurship that will grow,
- rewarding inventions, even if such inventions may compete with large vested interests,
- above all by setting a meaningful and adequate minimum wage for all employment for all workers of all ages, including the very young and inexperienced.

Libertarian Opportunities

Indeed, entrepreneurship could most easily be encouraged by freeing business from the protectionism of government restrictions. This could be achieved by passing libertarian laws enabling all entrepreneurs to use their land and property as they wish.

In some cases newly issued company shares are much in demand and expected to start trading at a premium. Such shares should always be lotteried off in small lots to the poor instead of being reserved for insiders and the favorite clients of large stockbrokers.

No one seems to have noticed that such small-lot lotteries would be in the best interests of diversification. This would prevent buildup of unstable power groups of large investors, always a threat to management.

Spend – Don't Hoard

Spend your way out of poverty has often been recommended. Hoarding is not investing - it is selfishness, a form of greed - the root of all evil. Investing is not just giving, it is informed giving in the hope of a fair future return.

There is an old proverb, "Cast your bread (your sustenance) upon the waters and it will return unto you after many days." Put another way, What goes around comes around. Investment and spending increases your standard of living and builds up savings which creates jobs which you and yours may one day need.

Stinginess or greed closes down the system. Give and it shall be given unto you. On the contrary, stinginess is a disease that is causing great poverty and misery in the world generally and in the poor world in particular.

It is the business manager's work to reverse this negative cycle into a positive drive towards more products, more services, more foods, at a lower cost and a higher standard of living for healthier and longer-lived, happier consumers.

Business needs a firm, consistent and orderly framework of money laws.

When your OUTGO is greater than your small INCOME – Then ALL your big upkeep will be your own DOWNFALL

CHAPTER NINETEEN
SOCIAL RIGHTS

In addition to the three R's (Reading, Writing and Arithmetic), employees often need access to instruction books, training manuals and basic courses to develop their skills. So,

- *What kind of training facilities are available near the trading area?*
- *Are there any problems with public transportation such as lack of buses, taxis or parking facilities?*
- *Is there an adequate supply of labor available locally.*
- *Can people establish co-ops without unnecessary restrictions?*

1 - Public Education

Business requires that public education respond to the need for actual social and vocational skills. Therefore, education should not be focused on the minute examination of academic theories.

Public education is one of the few results of government activity that gives the taxpayer value for money. This is so, because government is under pressure to train and educate everyone to their fullest potential. This training provides a well educated, skilled and competent body of workers for business owners to call on.

Only well paid workers can afford to buy goods and services on a regular and consistent basis. Only the healthy and well educated can be called upon to work for new employers in creative and innovative fields.

Vocational Training

Most business managers would prefer a good public school system that includes certain essentials such as free general education up to twelve years of age. Depending on the skills needed, this should be followed by free vocational education for teens up to nineteen years of age. Teens should be able to choose their options for vocational training. This would also include free school meals for all children with perhaps breakfasts, lunches and afternoon takeaway sandwiches.

Vocational education could lead to basic certification in some trades. At any such point youth could take up employment if they so wished.

After this, students could achieve certified status as technicians in various fields of employment. They would then be prepared to enter professional schools to obtain full licenses to practice in the professions such as but not limited to:

- law
- engineering
- accounting
- medical and health sciences
- hairdressing
- pharmacy
- translation (into English)
- navigation
- building and house repairs
- architecture

It is important that there should be no dead-end training. All vocational certifications, courses and diplomas should fit into modular subsections as part of overall training towards recognized qualifications.

All vocational and professional education should be provided free by publicly supported schools to all those who have passed the academic prerequisites at all levels. This would ensure flexibility in moving from one vocation to another - which is a great need of the modern civilized world.

Perhaps all those qualified by prerequisites should be given a chance to re-qualify if they wish every twenty years or so. This should be on the basis of merit only, without discrimination against creed, color or age.

Why should good workers be encouraged to retire on public funds? The older and weaker could re-qualify for less exacting careers. Nor is there any reason to discriminate against younger students who should be able to opt for their choice of vocational education from the age of thirteen, even if this means spending the school year in a vocational school away from home. Boarding schools should not be a privilege only for the rich, the few and the favored.

All professions should be open to merit on a career-long basis.

Governments should work towards the recognition of each others professional and technical qualifications at all levels. This would facilitate travel abroad and also international trade.

Many business managers would find it useful if free vocational education in practical skills was made available for people in all age groups.

The qualities needed to succeed in college are the same as those needed to succeed in real-life entrepreneurship:

- hard work
- good memory
- integrity and ability to argue the case clearly before class or in exams
- the ability to research and draw up fair statements and reports of what has been researched
- face-to-face communications in presentations of papers
- ability to gather and hand down specific information and form opinions from it
- getting along well with colleagues and professors who often judge a student's presentations and research

Under the system advocated, they would be guaranteed an opportunity to succeed in the most competitive of all human streets - the school.

More training should be directed towards self-employment and home employment rather than towards jobs and employees. Firms should at least partly train their own employees.

No longer should large pools of trained workless drive down wages at public expense. This robs business of a well paid recipient market for innovative goods and services. It leads to a peasant economy of a few haves and many have-nots.

Yet education is of no value unless it can be seen to have been carried out with integrity by both students and teachers. All exams should be videoed while in progress and kept on record, especially oral examinations.

2 - Land Reform

The essence of building up any economy is to fully utilize all natural resources, such as seas, waterways for fish, land for growth of food, rocks and mountains for mining.

In many parts of the world land is not fully utilized. Ideally, it should be made available to entrepreneurs who would be able to use it more productively.

A more efficient allocation of resources, based on consumer needs rather than vested landlord interests, would increase property values in the long run and also create jobs and tax revenue. As job creation continued, wages would also be bid up to higher levels. The result being increased general income producing even more tax revenues.

The greater production of goods and services resulting from land reform ensures that there would be less inflation in prices.

In short, there is likely to be a higher standard of living and more markets for business.

**People need a HAND UP in training for skills
Not a HAND OUT to the unskilled**

---

3 - A Pension

Pension rights are needed, not only to prevent hardship but also to ensure the buildup of receptive markets for new goods and services.

4 - Public Communications

Entrepreneurs need widespread public communications that is good and cheap, not only for their own personal use but for customers to contact them.

In some western countries local telephone calls are paid for separately in addition to the general telephone service charge and cost. Altogether, these local calls separately charged can come to a pretty penny.

In some nations the public must pay a lot of money just for a license to own a TV set and not all public payphones in booths can receive calls. Equipment such as TVs, PCs, handsets, even radios can cost twice as much as in other places.

In some nations, public payphone booths are few on the ground, highly likely to be vandalized and where available, expensive; the internet costs a fortune and payment will be accepted only by interest-bearing credit cards (no checks). Courier service is a high-cost luxury that only big companies can afford. Cable TV is often not widespread.

The business owner planning advertising campaigns or other marketing programs, needs to be aware of what is, or is not, readily and cheaply available before going into business in such places.

5 - Public Transit

The right to public transportation can make all the difference to a marketing plan. Customers, clients, visitors and theatre-goers must be able to visit the place of business, fairly easily and safely, at a reasonable cost. In many countries roads are overcrowded with cars and safe, nearby parking is unobtainable in some places.

Good transit systems are needed to relieve the commuter from the burden of pollution, smog, accidents and road rage. These could be by either bus, plane, cab, tram, chopper, train and boat. This would help to grease the wheels of business along with pedestrianized pedal-cycling, pedal-cabs and walking trails, nature trails, trains, ferries, choppers, hovercraft, railways and cable-cars.

Public transport is therefore a two-way street for entrepreneurs.

6 - Co-ops

> **Co-ops – groups of self-employed – could help to provide training for business managers.**

There should be clear incentives for the setting up of cooperatives either by consumers, wholesalers or producers. Such incentives could include tax breaks or land-leasing or special training.

The best use of national resources can be achieved by setting up co-ops such as:

- farmers' produce markets
- organic food sales
- crafts and jewelry
- visual arts like painting
- sculpture

as well as cooperative community-owned and operated farms, fishing boats and seafood gathering.

Participative management schemes, shared ownership programs and co-ops are all training for would-be entrepreneurs and all help to prepare the average person for their own individual entrepreneurial small business at a later date.

Those preparing to become full-grown business owners could benefit from free vocational training for all who have the prerequisites. This would provide help with promoting self-employment skills, traineeships, internships or business start-ups.

When companies move abroad, they often cannot take their plant, such as machinery and equipment. Governments at any level can then step in and buy the plant, tools, furniture, machines and so on. This plant often cannot be exported and may be on sale at a steep discount.

Governments can then help to set up co-ops for the laid-off local employees to operate. Local and labor groups may wish to help in setting up such co-ops. This could easily be mandated by government as a right and is one partial answer to unemployment.

Higher wages for the underpaid foreign worker would also help to eliminate unfair competition in industrialized societies. This would also create more entrepreneurial markets abroad for the things we grow or produce at home.

> **Co-ops for the building of cruise ships, ferries and cargo ships could help to provide much needed travel facilities for exports/imports, holidays and retirement.**

7 – Travel

> **Welfare states tend to restrict travel.**

The right to travel freely is essential for business. There should be no internal exile. Every citizen should have the right to a passport and the right to use it freely.

Of course, the welfare state is the main barrier to freedom of travel. Before the welfare state, people such as writers, scholars, artists, students, investors and entrepreneurs traveled freely - the assumption being that if they ran out of money they would return home or die on the spot at no cost to the host nation. Many continued to live abroad on their wits or by selling their skills on the open market. All this to the great enrichment of the country being visited.

Nowadays, some welfare states force travelers to prove that they have the means to live abroad for the rest of their lives or else curtail their visas to short stays. Very few people can prove that they have a guaranteed future income, so that the modern welfare system can drive out all foreigners on the grounds that they might dare to collect one or another state benefit or even a job.

Why could welfare states not simply agree to reciprocal benefits for temporary travelers? This would include recognition of each other's degrees, citizenship and qualifications and would greatly free the artist, writer and other professionals to travel. Or why not simply close down the welfare state and dismantle all its intrusive poking and prying into people's private business? That is, abolish all means testing.

> **Social institutions such as freedom to travel, free training, communications, adequate pensions and opportunities to enter business should all be harnessed for the needs of business – all to build up markets.**

CHAPTER TWENTY
JUDICIAL RIGHTS

- *Are all laws clearly defined or are some ambiguous?*
- *Can systematic and methodical conditions be applied to the business?*
- *Is the legal system fair?*
- *What legal obligations does a business have to follow in certain regions?*
- *Is a person considered innocent until proven guilty?*
- *Can a person be tried more than once for the same crime?*

These and many similar questions need to be considered by anyone thinking of going into business.

1- Presumption of Innocence

The right to be considered innocent until proven guilty is a complex one. In some industrialized countries the nation, that is the innocent taxpayer, routinely pays out direct compensation for the damage caused by the guilty.

This appears to be a violation of the presumption of innocence but in fact the business may well benefit from this misplaced compensation. It is like receiving automatic insurance for some crimes.

It should be noted that private insurance is also widely available to bet against most wrongs caused by lawbreakers – burglary, theft, forgery, arson and stolen identities.

However, business managers may consider that this compensation represents a general attitude of government interference which may be less favorable to business in other respects. Here, government is the presiding 'big daddy'.

The devil is in the detail –
Beware of the 'small print' **in government regulations**

---

2 - Equality

Every citizen should have equal right of access to taxpayer supported goods, services and privileges such as safety, security, utilities, land, libraries, law and order, hygiene, college courses, degrees, certifications, licenses to trade/business, public jobs. Everyone should have equal access to these facilities.

In some countries, the constitutional situation is lawless and erratic discretion. Indeed, in one or two places there is at present no constitution, written or unwritten, to protect a business.

3 – Laws of Fairness

The most basic aspect of laws of fairness is that everyone should be treated equally before the law. If any discrimination occurs against anyone, it is irrelevant if that was not the original intention.

Discrimination is discrimination.

The road to hell is paved with good intentions. Law cannot deal in mind reading.

There should be a ban on double jeopardy and no person should be tried more than once for the same crime.

All persons found guilty of any crime should have an automatic right of appeal to state and central courts of appeal. Appeals to higher courts should be automatic and not subject to discretionary rulings by lower courts.

> **Discretion is an open invitation to bribery and corruption.**

Fair laws are unlikely to be passed in the absence of strong, secure and stable government. In many nations, the following business law reforms should be considered:

1. Each litigant should be responsible for legal fees - win or lose. At present, in some nations, large institutions and groups can run up huge legal expenses. This almost ensures that the richest side will win. If the case is lost, the poorer litigant is often expected to pay these enormous expenses. This acts as a deterrent to the little guy to bring the case in the first place. Loser pays sounds good but is antidemocratic and unjust since the little guy is usually the loser who cannot afford justice.

2. Defendants should not be expected to prove their whereabouts on any given date more than two or three years past. Therefore, since so many innocent persons are being found guilty, there should be a statute of limitations of 10 years on all crimes. This limitation should be imposed not according to the seriousness of the crime which is irrelevant but on the basis of the ability of the court and jury to reach a fair conclusion after a period of many years.

In particular, eyewitness evidence does not age well. Those accused of serious crimes should have the choice of trial by jury or by a tribunal of three judges who should be qualified in business law and be practicing lawyers or accountants.

Given modern methods of DNA detection proofs, forensic science, cash and credit travel records, a 10-year statute of limitations on all crimes should be time enough to solve crimes. This would force society to act more quickly in catching criminals.

4 - Fair Trials

This right covers the freedom to have full due process with traditional safeguards for all persons who have been arrested and charged or served with a writ under civil law.

It includes the following rights:
- to full disclosure of all evidence to both prosecution and defense councils
- to call witnesses
- present evidence freely
- obtain reasonable bail in non-violent cases
- impartiality on the part of judge and jury

In particular, it should be unlawful to make payments in cash or kind to witnesses in criminal cases.

Witnesses of bad repute should not be allowed to testify in court. It should be clear that fellow jailbirds often try to pander to police and jailers by giving evidence of alleged confessions on the part of the accused. Such testimony should be totally unacceptable as well as the testimony of any witness who has been befriended, rewarded or supported by any police or government agency.

Witnesses should be impartial and stand to gain nothing by testimony. There should be no secret laws or regulations.

If any person confesses (whether orally or in writing) to a crime that they did not commit, that person should be considered guilty of the crime of aiding and abetting a criminal to escape.

5 - Victim's Compensation

Criminals should be totally responsible for their crimes and their earnings and assets should be garnished to repay the victim. The criminal should not profit from his crime by having the taxpayer pay out compensation to the victims.

Criminals should not be allowed to directly profit from their crimes by making films, interviews or writing books or articles based on their crimes.

Another form of reward funded by the taxpayer is for the state to present criminals with a new identity to help them hide from those whom they have wronged. Criminals, as opposed to innocent informants, should not be so rewarded at public expense.

Victims, direct and indirect, should be able to sue criminals under a variety of torts. Victims should also be able to claim for straightforward compensation.

People should have a right to know if child killers, thieves, muggers or other criminals are living in their neighborhood. For this reason, criminals should be readily identifiable.

Modern banking technology easily enables all stolen monies to be removed from the accounts or other assets of the thief by court-ordered direct debit and transferred to the victim's personal bank account.

6 - Free Courts

Accountants and lawyers can usually be relied upon to resolve any ambiguities and inconsistencies which often occur in business situations.   However, readily available courts should be the last resort for universal justice.

7 - Accountable Governments

Entrepreneurs, business managers, as well as lawmakers, should all be held financially accountable for any professional malpractice.

Public auditing offices, staffed by fully qualified accountants, should be maintained at all three levels of government. Their purpose would be to scrutinize all finances of publicly listed limited companies and to oversee all work carried out by all persons receiving public funds. Such accountants should not merely carry out annual audits.   To be effective, they would need to be employed on an ongoing, continuous basis.

**Business managers should be
held responsible for their mistakes
as well as being rewarded for their successes**

**Law courts should be designed
to include business laws and fairness**

CHAPTER TWENTY ONE
PERSONAL RIGHTS

It is necessary to consider a number of personal and personality issues.

- *Can a person start a business from their own home?*
- *If so, what kind of legal restrictions would have to be addressed?*
- *Is there a right to self-defense?*
- *Is there a culture of self-reliance?*

1 - Buy a Home

It is important that business activity should be spread as widely as possible throughout the community. In many cases home ownership is the first step for the setting up of a home-based business.

Landlords almost universally object to tenants using their home as a base for business. This occurs even where other legal requirements have been met. Therefore, it is always a good idea to give house tenants a right to buy their own home.

All tenants of either private or public homes who live in such dwellings as their sole habitation should have the right to purchase their home from their landlord. This should be at fair and current market value. This would tend to move some small but useful capital from passive landlordism to other public or private business investments.

The right to buy should apply to dwellings or domiciles only, not to farms. There are plenty of other property investments besides personal home ownership which can be used by the landlord for commercial purposes.

These properties include:
- Blocks of offices
- Restaurants and cafes
- Blocks of garages
- Parking spaces with meters
- Streets of retail stores
- Extensive sets of allotments
- Small farms
- Small factories
- Industrial units

The right to home ownership is an important foundation of business startups. An alternative to this option would be laws that give the tenant rights of tenure to engage in a home business.

Home owners should not be subject to eminent domain except where homes stand in the way of a major public development such as a main road, a school or a library.

2 – Ownership of Assets

This is the right to own goods, chattels, land, buildings, investments of all kinds including abstract or intellectual property. This is a basic prerequisite for business ownership.

In general, property ownership - real, personal or intellectual - is the basis of a free market system. However, some but not many countries have recently rescinded this basic and longstanding right in favor of seizure upon suspicion of criminality.

New businesses should avoid setting up in such places, as these laws lend themselves to discretionary confiscation.

> **Discretionary confiscation amounts to seizing assets according to anyone's guess**

3 - Self-Defense

The right of self-defense should include:
- the right to bear small arms or other defensive

gear such as weapons, vehicles, sprays or dog-repellants

- the freedom to wear bullet-proof or other protective clothing, shoes, gloves, helmets at all times and on all occasions
- the right to defend one's person and property as well as friends, family, home and grounds.

In cases where attackers, muggers or intruders suffer injury when being repelled, there should be an absolute and unequivocal immunity from civil or criminal proceedings against the self-defender.

It is irrelevant whether there is any injury suffered by the attacker. It is also irrelevant whether the self-defense was excessive.

The point is that there is a greater problem that lawsuits and charges against self-defenders encourages predators to attack in the belief that they enjoy the protection of the law. It should be clear that they do not enjoy the care, succor and support of society in the course of their thefts.

In short, such lawsuits against the victims of violence encourages more violence against innocent persons - especially those who are known to have a little money, such as farmers or small business persons.

4 – Ownership of Ideas

It is almost impossible to steal an idea, yet many people try and, to the very slight extent that they succeed, a great deal of damage is caused to both the originator of the idea and to the idea itself.

It is important to define what is in the people's common copyright known as the public domain.

Almost all the great classics over the centuries have been based on stories and facts in the public domain.

In most nations, new books, movies, audios or videos can be based on material in the public domain without any infringement of copyright.

Material in the public domain should preferably be listed, defined and clarified so that it can be developed and extended as much as possible in order to enrich the culture of the people.

At the same time, in the opposite direction, there should be protection of new ideas. Systematic steps towards improvements in quality of life need to be protected by law to ensure that innovators can be rewarded.

Theft of Ideas

Attempts made to steal ideas almost always fail. This is because an idea is a unique creation. It is like the top piece of a pyramid which requires support from increasingly larger numbers of sub-ideas. These are necessary in order to hold up the top piece of the pyramid. Those who try to steal top-of-pyramid ideas can rarely, if ever, build down the rest of the ever broader and broadening base of ideas necessary to hold up that top piece. So it is that the original idea topples and falls to the ground. This damages the innovator by bringing the fallen idea into disrepute.

Protection of Ideas

Ideas should always be well protected in order to encourage the typical ideas-rich entrepreneur.

A civil service department should be responsible for registering or patenting new ideas free of charge. Otherwise, poor inventors will need to sell their ideas to big corporations who alone will be able to patent them, sell them or suppress them.

Protection should be automatic and not call for fees or further formalities to encourage a free-flow of what is, after all, the basis of all business progress.

5 - Public Healthcare

Needed healthcare should be provided from birth to grave for all legal or illegal residents within a nation's borders. This should, of course, include all drug treatment, medicine, physical treatment and psychological counseling needed by the patient.

All treatment should be by qualified and experienced therapists of the patient's choice. Such a national health system should not preclude private healthcare practitioners. The extra cost should be agreed between the patient and the practitioner.

Preventive Healthcare

A free healthcare national system is a good investment for business. Although with added private practice supplementation it could become very expensive.

**If employees are not healthy
they will be unable to work at their best.**

Therefore, it will always be necessary to have public preventative healthcare and planning in favor of a healthy lifestyle.

This should include required healthy food education in all schools and colleges with adherence to strict codes of practice for all food producers and servicers.

An excellent idea would be the provision of about three, free healthy meals each day for school children of all ages. Another good idea would be to discourage the use of all refined or bleached grains and have them classified as eligible for VAT or other special taxes.

Only in this way can business firms be sure of a dependable workforce that is healthy and intelligent.

Governments sharing at all three levels - central, state or county – should provide all basic and generalist healthcare free of charge.

Private or public colleges should be accredited to be able to examine and offer certification and licenses to those graduates who qualify as healthcare practitioners.

There is no need for any government exclusives in any field of therapy which should be open to all qualified healthcare entrepreneurs.

6 - Human Self-Reliance

Business owners should search out regions that respect self-reliance. For it is only in such civilized environments that business can be made to flourish.

Handouts and doles are not the solution to human poverty and misery.

Rather, some of the main answers are education, training or apprenticeships and opportunities for fair employment in the public as well as the private sector.

The principle here is:
from each according to his ability,
to each according to his contribution to society.

---

7 - Individual Choices

Choices of supplier or demander are the essence of entrepreneurship and business. The right to choose is fundamental to a free market system. This includes the right to choose:

- what foods to buy
- what clothes to wear
- where to live and shop
- what transportation to use
- which books to read

- not to be constrained by prohibition of drinks, drugs or food as selected for us by our superiors

Prohibitions

Such constraints on our freedom of choice are known as prohibitions. Prohibitions are complex in moral, physical and economic terms. They need to be clearly analyzed by the business manager.

In fact, all prohibitions appear to be deliberately designed to create a profitable black market for insiders.

Successful entrepreneurship needs much libertarian freedom of choice for both business manager and customer-client and supplier for the setting up of free buying and selling.

In short, for successful business to be carried on, the purveyors of land, labor, capital and entrepreneurship all need free access to each other.

> **Personal rights to come and go and to set up businesses can be developed into opportunities to trade – such as a part-time home business.**

CHAPTER TWENTY TWO
SUMMARY

This book has presented an introductory outline of the basics of business economics.

Chapter One discussed the creation of business firms and the business-friendly political framework which needs to define the legal and structured environment.

CommonWealthism is defined as a system of free markets encouraging:

- entrepreneurship,
- small business,
- co-ops,
- partnerships,

and other small and medium-sized businesses as compared to socialism or capitalism.

Chapter Two discussed the basic idea of the child's swopshop as a model for business - that is, a place where exchanges take place to suit the needs of both buyer and seller.

The chapter also introduced the four factors of production: land, labor, capital and entrepreneurship or business management.

Summary

Chapter Three described how a market is a place where goods (including services) are bought and sold. Arbitrage being the result of moving goods or services from one place (where they are cheap) to another place (where they are more expensive). To be valuable a good must be rare or scarce.

Chapter Four looked at the laws of supply and demand which set out the basic tendency that buyers will buy more at lower prices and suppliers will supply more at higher prices.

Chapter Five discussed the equilibrium point. This is the point at which goods are sold so that the sale is satisfactory to both buyer and seller. It is the place where the shelves are clear in the store - all the goods have been sold - i.e., there are no shortages or surpluses and no one is asking for the goods who is prepared to pay a dollar or even a penny more than the equilibrium price.

Chapter Six discussed inflation and deflation. When money generally buys less over a sustained period of time, this is called inflation.

Since inflation is a general rise in the level of prices, it follows that only governments can cause inflation. Individual producers can only produce shortages or over-supply of their own goods or services. Only governments are big enough to increase or decrease the supply of money to the extent that it results in inflation or deflation.

Governments do this by:

1. printing money and giving it to businesses and employees in exchange for goods and services;
2. introducing bylaws, taxes and tariffs that reduce the supply of products relative to the money in circulation;
3. issuing bonds and paying out fixed rates of interest on these bonds over different periods of time.
4. by setting the interest rates charged by the central bank for commercial loans.

Shortages are also caused by governments going to war.

The opposite of inflation is deflation. This occurs when money becomes more valuable due to its decreasing supply. When there is not enough money in circulation for people to buy what they need, money increases in value.

Chapters Seven and Eight noted that money is worth what people think it is worth. No more or no less.

A Government Money Wheel can be thought of as government spending and income. This is where government takes in taxes and borrows (or prints) money, then sends the money out by way of spending and handouts and wages and pensions to government employees and others. This money then enters the economy by way of spending and investing through banks, stocks and bonds and brokers and businessmen.

As the money enters the economy it reproduces its effect by passing from one spender to another. This percolating of money through the economic system is known as the Multiplier Effect. For business to succeed and that also means, all in all, for any economy to grow, the four factors of production must all be working together.

Chapter Nine outlined the fact that circumstances such as climate, fashion, laws, culture, general health, religion - almost any factor except price and quantity - creates a totally different market.

 Chapter Ten talked about the money growth-upwards theory which holds that wealth grows upwards and generally does not trickle down as many modern economists have mistakenly believed. The growth-upwards theory is that as entrepreneurs make profits at lower levels they spend the money in developing higher markets.

Chapter Eleven looked at the Pyramid of Profits which consisted of the four levels of markets, i.e., Basic, Service, Luxury and Higher-level markets. The top levels, even the middle levels of this pyramid, cannot exist unsupported - in mid-air. Therefore it makes no sense to try to stimulate business at a higher level until there is full support for that level at all the lower levels. That is why many third world countries are in a state of collapse even after large sums have been thrown at their higher levels.

In weak markets, these higher levels lack the support of profits and high standard of living drifting up from owners, managers and workers at the lower levels. In such part-markets there are not enough consumers with money at the lower level to support the higher levels.

Instead of giving money to level one small industry - poverty banks and farmers markets, artisans and tradesmen, craftsmen, builders then architects, accountants, schools of craft and trade and so on, money has been thrown at politicians and big business people and institutions before society has the upgoing funds and customers to support these higher institutions.

The poor first, then the small business classes should have been the cry and the sequence of economic aid. These in turn would have created and built up and supported the higher level institutions.

The middle and lower levels must be put in place if the top of the pyramid is to succeed in trickling down any wealth. In short, wealth must grow upwards before it can trickle down.

Chapter Twelve suggested that business plans and predictions should be based on Socioeconomic models designed only to give general future trends rather than precise mathematical models designed to predict precise results. Statistics – yes. Mathematics - no.

Chapter Thirteen outlined Fifteen Conditions Favorable to Economic Growth:

1. The Limited Company - No share owner should be personally responsible for the debts of the company.

2. Laws of Debt Recovery - so that even small firms should get paid what is owed to them.

3. Right to Do Business - without government permission.

4. Lower Taxes - people will work harder if they can keep more of their own money.

5. Freedom of Labor - free rights of skilled labor to enter and leave the country and move freely within the economy.

6. No Restrictions on Business Closure - Such restrictions were conceived to protect labor from layoffs but act only as a disincentive for entrepreneurs to hire labor in the first place.

7. Law and Order - the rule of law keeps down predators such as extortioners, robbers, thieves, burglars, blackmailers, confidence tricksters, false advertisers and embezzlers. Business needs the freedom for customers to walk the streets.

8. Freedom to Move Capital - capital goods and currency need to move in and out of any

country or region. Established business or entrepreneurs will not send capital in, if they know that they cannot take it out later.

9. Good Educational Systems - good workers must have technical skills, computer-savvy and literacy.

10. Good Wages for All - people must be well paid in order to create markets for goods.

11. Fair Civil Laws - No economic region or country can afford a court which seeks to achieve popularity by penalizing business.

12. Free and Good Communications - Internet, phone, fax, mail, TV, cable and broadcast radio and print should all be free of government control or ownership.

13. Good Transit Systems - Canals, roads, rivers, seaways, rail, air, tunnels fit for trains, cable cars, cars, trucks, boats, barges, cargo planes, trains, bicycles and taxis.

14. Mass Spread of Investments - good investments set up by government or firms should be widely available.

15. Interest Rates - should be fair to savers as well as to borrowers since savings are in part used by banks to lend needed capital to entrepreneurs who create jobs.

Chapter Fourteen looked at the specific business rights and conditions needed for successful business planning.

Chapter Fifteen - Moral Freedoms:

1. <u>Free Speech</u> - speaking out truth and sincere opinion.
2. <u>Free Press</u> - all media, video, film, audio, radio, books, Internet.
3. <u>Walk</u> - assemble, demonstrate, protest and petition and not be arrested or subjected to threats.
4. <u>Receive the Truth</u> - receive information, to read, to know consumer facts.
5. <u>Religion</u> - to practice, with a full separation of church and state.
6. <u>Effective Spending of Taxes</u> - No overseas aid, except in kind. Money sent overseas goes astray. Honest administration of taxes. Good use of taxes, supporting no favorites - no privileged persons or groups.
7. <u>Meritocracy</u> - all public appointments should to be made on written, objective and anonymously-graded qualifications. Efficient administration of all laws.

Chapter Sixteen - Security Freedoms

1. <u>Auditing of Public Purse</u> - Checks on all public monies. Audits of all spending by fully qualified accountants.
2. <u>Law and Order</u> - Codes of criminal law, police militias, special volunteer cops. Code of business law.
3. <u>Liberty and Life</u> - Habeas Corpus. Pursuit of happiness. A culture of no kidnapping.
4. <u>Peace at Home and Abroad</u> – For the orderly conduct of business.
5. <u>Privacy</u> - No searches or bugs without probable cause, i.e., prima facie evidence of a crime. No special branch or political police. Privacy at home.
6. <u>Integration</u> - In housing and jobs - no attacks from ghettos. A one race policy towards a worldwide human melting pot.
7. <u>Personal Protection</u> - no torture, cruelty, severe punishment, death penalty, police beatings.

Chapter Seventeen - Political Freedoms

1. <u>Citizenship</u> - right to live and reside where one can own, sell or exchange or buy.
2. <u>Checks and Balances</u> - of power, as between head of government and the rest of government.
3. <u>Fair Voting</u> - Referendums, elections and the right to vote.
4. <u>Three Levels of Bicameral Governments</u> - county, state and central.
5. <u>Direct Choice of Leaders</u> - Regular two-year election of all senior civil officers.
6. <u>Equal Press Time</u> - A fair press. Obligations on press to act as critics or provide ideas. No state-owned media. Fair, equal time and print space for political opponents.
7. <u>Recall of Failures</u> - to fire all elected, if they fail to keep promises. A system for recalling all public officers.

Chapter Eighteen - Financial Freedoms

1. <u>Good Wages</u> - to create stability and good markets for business. Minimum wages should be set by law.
2. <u>Do Business</u> - more jobs for all (including limited company formation to limit liability).
3. <u>Free Market Economy</u> - Capital use. No state monopolies, or over-interference in business. Protection of business savings critical mass.
4. <u>Fair Taxes</u> - No billeting. Taxes as low as needed to keep infrastructure sound and secure.
5. <u>Fair Interest Rates</u> - to lenders and borrowers.
6. <u>Receive Debts Owed</u> - to get paid what is owed. Use of garnishee orders rather than punishment of debtors.
7. <u>Fair Shares for All</u> - spread of investments - fair shares - for all workers and the public. Encourage betweentaking. No unfairly restrictive zoning or planning regulations.

Chapter Nineteen – Social Rights

1. <u>Public Education</u> - Exams to be monitored and graded by those who do not know the examinee.   Training at all levels to be provided free to all who qualify.
2. <u>Land</u> - to be owned by individuals in small lots.   State land to be lotteried off to the landless.
3. <u>Pensions</u> - to all legal residents on basis of age - to support markets.
4. <u>Public Communications </u> - phone, radio, mail, TV, internet. Free local calls, free email.
5. <u>Public Transit</u> - taxis, ferries, planes, canals, buses, boats, copters, trains.
6. <u>Co-ops</u> - the right of customers and workers to set up co-ops. Participative management and ownership. The right to form a worker, customer or producer co-op. The right of workers or customers at retail or producer co-ops to buy shares in equity-sharing and ownership schemes.
7. <u>Travel and Relocation</u> - Freedom of movement within or outside the nation with no internal exile.

Chapter Twenty - Judicial Freedoms

1. <u>Innocence</u> - No internment or assumption of guilt without proof. The right not to pay, thru taxes, compensation for injuries caused by another. No need to prove one's innocence.

2. <u>Equality</u> - No bribery or financial support for politicians. Equality before the law for all.

3. <u>Fair and Open Laws</u> - Right to juries. Freedom from double jeopardy or legal harassment. No secret laws.

4. <u>Fair Trials</u> - Due process. Right of appeal. Community votes on legal officials such as prosecuting attorneys and judges. Recall or indictments if a substantial petition is made.

5. <u>Victims' Compensation</u> - only from the perpetrators of the crime and on a garnishee basis. Victims should not need to sue.

6. <u>Free Court System</u> - presided over by elected experts including a constitutional court to preside over public rights and to review and advise on laws but only occasionally to overrule the legislature or the civil service who, in any case, should normally control the purse.

7. <u>Accountable Government</u> - subject to laws setting out financial responsibility for mistakes or corruption.

Chapter Twenty One - Personal Rights

1. <u>Buy a Home</u> - Rights for tenants and taxpayer help with mortgages for the poor, again to boost markets.

2. <u>Ownership of Goods, Chattels and Property</u> The right to ownership.

3. <u>Self Defense</u> - the right to bear arms, form neighborhood volunteers, local special policemen and legal representatives.

4. <u>Ideas</u> - ownership and protection of all intellectual property.

5. <u>Public Health</u> - national medical care and public hygiene for all.

6. <u>Brotherhood</u> - basic needs should be met in kind. No one should be dependent on humiliating cash handouts. Human dignity should be maintained as well as hygienic and humane conditions in all public and private works.

7. <u>Free Choices</u> - in matters of food, medicine, marriage, jobs, reading, viewing and spare time activities including political and entertainment.

***

Summary

**You will never know a man
until you do business with him**

Some libertarian freedoms and choices could be guaranteed by a Bill of Business Rights for business owners. This would set up a political economy that would encourage the growth of jobs, incomes, investments, tax growth and wealth. This could all lead to a higher standard, at a lower cost of living for everyone.

Every country in the world should ideally incorporate into its written constitution all those wide range of libertarian freedoms necessary for the individual to become self-employed and to create prosperity for all. This should help to meet the needs of others including those in distant and troubled lands.

A basic need of business owners is for a written charter for economic rights, freedoms and choices which are guaranteed as by a written and clear constitution. These rights should not be taken away by any branch of government at any level - local, state or central.

The Floating 50th libertarian economic freedom may be said to be the Rule of Law. In fact, the 50th Freedom is the general right to a Bill of Rights to a clear, simple written constitution as an underpinning for all the economy.   This will:

1. restrict what governments can or cannot do to the business owner (or the customer, producer, supplier for that matter).

2. define the limits of law so that one can live and go about one's lawful business progressively under fewer and better laws. This would achieve a higher standard of living at a lower cost. This could lead to a more predictable future, creating jobs, wealth, health, long life and happiness for more people.

Just what, precisely, in the way of a political framework - an economic infrastructure - a political economy, in a word - freedoms - does the businessman need? Well, obviously this is a matter of opinion, and opinions legitimately differ.

However, in the opinion and in the experience of this author who has written on entrepreneurship for over four decades the 49 above-listed rights/freedoms are sufficient.

Business owners should migrate to where these freedoms occur in any part of the globe.

Summary

This should be done before those freedoms are closed down by rulers who wish to sell the licenses for their own gain. The above is a list of seven times seven - 49 basic human rights which should help the business manager or entrepreneur to make rational decisions.

―――――

www.ingramcontent.com/pod-product-compliance
Lightning Source LLC
Chambersburg PA
CBHW032303210326
41520CB00047B/941